AN IDEAL BOY

FIRST AID IN ACCIDENTS

for fracture of the fore-arm

for the arm

Knee Bandage

Hip Bandage

Jaw Bandage

for poisonous bites

for fire Accidents

for water Accidents

FRIENDS OFFSET CALENDARS, 39, BUNDER STREET, MADRAS-1. PH: 5894

AN IDEAL BOY

Charts from India

Sirish Rao
V. Geetha
Gita Wolf

dewi lewis publishing
in association with tara publishing

TYPE OF ROCKS

IGNEOUS ROCK

VOLCANIC ERUPTION

SEDIMENTARY ROCK

METAMORPHIC ROCK

A SHARP ROCK

A LAYERED ROCK

A SMALL ROCK

A BIG ROCK

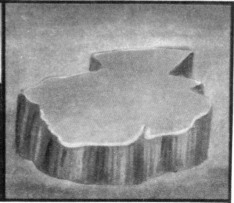

A SMOOTH ROCK

INTRODUCING CHARTS

The Indian market is full of educational charts on every imaginable subject. They cost almost nothing and are found everywhere, from tiny booths to large stationery shops. With a curious innocence, they combine text and images – often with bold and unapologetic disregard for veracity – to create a mix of stylised popular art and sanctimonious pedagogy, that can be startling to the outsider.

Designed and produced for the classroom, charts are used most widely in the poorer state-run schools. With almost non-existent resources, teachers buy them as cheap, easily assimilable educational aids to meet the requirements of a curriculum which demands students retain and recall enormous amounts of information.

But information is not all they provide. Charts are just as concerned with ethics and correct behaviour, insisting on codes of conduct, and narrating cautionary tales with suitable warnings. This stern didacticism – bordering on piety – is very much part of educational practice in India.

Perhaps this is why they are completely unremarkable to most Indians. Those who actually use them accept them as a matter of course. Others – particularly privileged Indians – simply have vague recollections of having come across them.

We have collected them since childhood, and for us charts possess a deep, inexplicable charm, quite separate from their use or status. The delight lies in their art, their unwitting humour and outrageously confident interpretations of reality. They are familiar, yet always startlingly fresh.

Charts are a dynamic part of Indian popular sensibility. It is in this light that we present this first survey of a remarkable form. This book features some of the best examples that we have collected and enjoyed. Sadly, it also documents an art-form bound to fade away in the age of the computer. Older hand-drawn charts are already being retouched and flattened by image editors, whilst many new ones use poor photography and homogenous clip art.

Selected from a collection of over one thousand, the examples in this book are not intended as an exhaustive documentation. They have found their way in on the basis of the richness of their art and content. But we wanted more than an assemblage of wonderful charts.

Although they can be enjoyed without interpretation, we felt the need to present them in context. There is an increasing tendency towards a fashionable appropriation of Indian kitsch and popular art. As authors from within the culture, we did not want to feed into a kind of celebratory postmodern orientalism. And so part of our concern was to locate charts within a living, material culture and to grant them and their makers the contexts within which to situate their meanings. This is fairly unmapped theoretical terrain, and we have sought as many founded locations as possible from which richer readings can emerge.

At the same time, we did not want to 'explain' the charts. The information provided is more a background against which to interpret them. For the reader who wants to know more, there are the longer historical essays at the end of the book.

As we went through our collection certain patterns became clear. Out of the possible ways of grouping them, we chose to identify overarching themes that held a particular set of charts together. What led our approach was not so much any clearly intentioned agenda on the part of the chart makers, as particular structures of feeling that a group of charts communicated.

Science is clearly important, going by the number of charts on birds, animals, natural processes, and the fascination of technology. Civics and moral science also appear significant both in terms of range and variety. A third group celebrates all things Indian, and another deals with the wonders of the world. The last section features miscellaneous charts broadly focusing on leisure.

This is the basis for the sections which follow, but the categories are not mutually exclusive. Charts that appear to belong to a certain sequence could just as easily go into another and so the thematic arrangement we have devised is not absolute.

Sirish Rao
V. Geetha
Gita Wolf

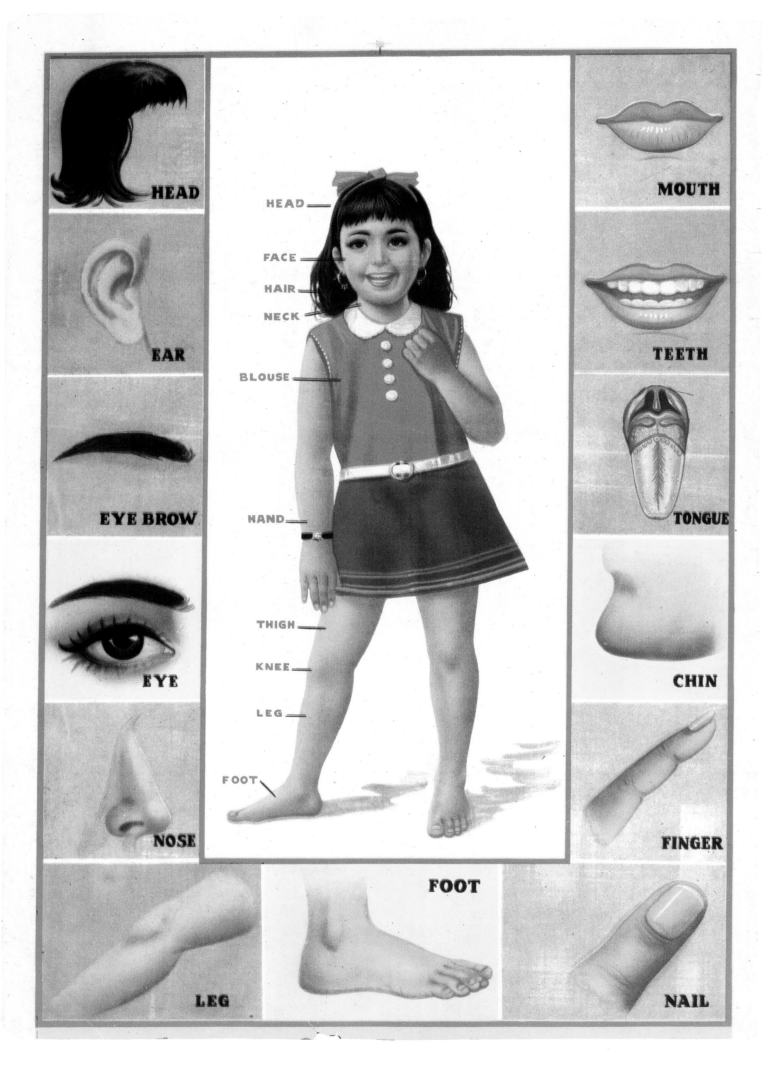

HEAD

EAR

EYE BROW

EYE

NOSE

LEG

HEAD
FACE
HAIR
NECK

BLOUSE

HAND

THIGH

KNEE

LEG

FOOT

FOOT

MOUTH

TEETH

TONGUE

CHIN

FINGER

NAIL

6

READING CHARTS

Educational charts came into the market in this form around the 1950s, when young teachers in independent India needed cheap teaching aids. Strictly speaking, their purpose is functional. Their content is largely based on state school curricula, with most themes connected to specific textbook lessons. However, it is not unusual to find the same theme rendered very differently when a chart is re-printed, so that particular versions become rare almost overnight.

Charts are published in English as well as in local languages, though the English charts are more widely available and preferred, even in schools teaching through another language. Since their strongest element is the visual, students often read them purely as pictures, with the teacher providing a rough translation.

Charts address the two basic pedagogical axes of the Indian educational system: the need for facts, and the need for moral instruction. In both cases, pupils across age groups (from five to fourteen) must organise information into simple, tabular formats. Chart publishers – sometimes assisted by teachers – respond to this, taking their cues from actual examination questions. The varied and sometimes puzzling categories of people, places, animals, birds, objects, human behaviour, activities and habits, are all part of a repertoire of knowledge made easy.

It is hard to overlook the fact that this large – and often bizarre – collection of ideas and information is unlikely to be particularly useful in forming meaningful concepts, and too abstract to assimilate in any real sense. Information exists as half understood categories, almost as a superstition. Children learn to memorise facts as they would a magic chant.

There is an element of poignancy here, which inevitably complicates the viewer's complete enjoyment of the charts' brilliant innocence. In a way, they are a sadly accurate mirror of the mass of Indian state education, pushed to a logical, absurd extreme.

And yet that does not quite encompass chart art. There is a happy energy to the form, and it has to do with something wonderful that happens along the way, in the slapdash rendering of information as it passes from textbook to chart. The art needs to be illustrative, yet its aesthetic energy has such a life of its own that it is never entirely subsumed by function. Through the chart artist, himself a product of this educational system, it resounds with the life-affirming and vibrant energy of the Indian streets.

The confused educational ideologies that the charts embody, their political naivety, their essential semantic innocence, all combine to transform the original theme in completely unexpected ways. Chart artists are generally not literate in English, though a large number of the charts they create are in this language. Sometimes, phrases are directly translated from the local language, resulting in quaint and delightful Indianisms. Through such mutations and personal interpretations, unforgivable misinformation found in Indian textbooks takes on a whimsical edge, as it passes through several hands during the process of chart making.

Chart publishers see their endeavour as primarily commercial, although they retain an old-world sense of the social worth of educational work. They will choose a theme and commission an artist for a particular chart, with clear and specific instructions on what to include. As work progresses, the artist, the publisher, the assistant, the platemaker and the printer all add their own interpretations. And so, like a Chinese whisper, the relationship of the end product to the original is complex. A chart is not a mere re-ordering of textbook facts; it is an imaginative redeploying of them, by literally anyone who is confident of doing so.

In the process, information is treated with such a cheerful lack of respect that charts can be read almost as a deconstruction of the knowledge business. They pass over spelling mistakes and incorrect labeling – either through carelessness or a genuine lack of knowledge. Ironically, they communicate a glorious irreverence for the very knowledge they exhort us to take seriously, without the slightest effort at an aesthetic or political self-consciousness. Ignorant of their own social and political implications, charts subvert the pedagogy they serve in unintended ways.

This is perhaps an important clue in reading and understanding charts as popular communication. They are entirely unselfconscious, so that mining them for social meanings always risks giving them an ideological coherence they do not possess. Chart artists do not consciously parody or subvert, nor do they push traditions to their limits. They take from the knowledge system available to them, returning their own version back into the same space. And so any criticism of content or educational value cannot really be directed at the artists or the publishers. It is the larger system that is at fault, and a critique of chart content is really a critique of structure.

HELPS OTHERS

1. Do'nt Throw Sweepings & Fruit-peels.

THE ART OF THE CHARTS

An awareness of the background from which the charts come is a way of going beyond reading them as purely humourous kitsch. They are certainly funny, but there is a richer world here, filled with a very authentic energy that is moving in the way it actively participates in a larger structure it had little power to create. This energy deserves both attention and affection. It has the limitations of a flawed structure, but its very presence in this form points to an active democratic appropriation of voice and space.

The most significant thing about popular communication in India is the nature of the society it addresses: grossly unequal and largely illiterate, on one hand, and assuredly democratic on the other. Charts reflect this relationship brilliantly, by combining the semi-literacy of an unequal society with the mordant energy of a lively polity.

In a largely non-literate society, the visual takes on a certain potency. But there is no easy slot into which chart art fits, and it seems to incorporate elements of several popular art forms simultaneously.

There are certainly several aspects here that would fit into Western theories of kitsch. Charts simulate knowledge for easy consumption, much as kitsch objects simulate the aesthetic experience without actually having to struggle with it. Mass-produced, derivative, and clearly not original they also draw information and visual input from a variety of sources, making generous use of ideal homes, sweet children and buxom women.

And yet, despite all this, they contain something that kitsch, by its very definition, does not – the individual hand of the maker. Even as the chart artist makes use of existing stereotypical images, the language of the visual cliché never succeeds in completely defining his creation. Charts break out of the homogeneity of kitsch all the time, sometimes through reckless semantic errors, but also, more importantly, through the characteristic individuality of the particular artist.

Ironically though almost all these artists are nameless. The typical chart artist is usually a self-taught commercial artist, whose work includes magazine illustration, signboards, calendars, or cinema hoardings. Charts tend to rank low in this scale of urban graphic art, perhaps because they have neither the visibility nor the flamboyance of other street forms.

Chart art can be broadly classified as naive, though the artist here does not attempt to create his own view of the world, so much as respond – using the visual language he is familiar with – to a specific brief. He needs to follow a particular visual grid, creating panels of images that together make up a chart. Like a comic strip, each panel is treated as a distinct unit yet exists as a part of the whole, both visually and thematically. This requires well honed skills to narrate, communicate, and at the same time balance the composition.

GOOD MANNERS AT HOME

At the Shop.

WEL COME   The School Fair

MANNERS AT HOME

Working broadly within the codes of naive art, artists are wonderfully eclectic at absorbing all kinds of styles and sources. In this sense, they link to a long tradition of urban graphic art, going as far back as the 18th century. Elements of the so-called Company Art of colonial India, for example, are still evident in the way the people of India are visualised. Settings and draperies are inspired by the backdrops of calendar art and early films, and the Caucasian looking children they favour appear to be drawn from early European advertising and magazine art.

But these conventions are re-worked even as they are used. Generally, artists are more concerned with successful narrative than realistic depiction, and visual codes are read as a language that signifies, rather than represents. It is a dialogue between given models and an active imagination that comes closest to defining the art of the charts. Artists play with form almost as a matter of course, some more generous with the play impulse than others. The art communicates because it uses stereotypes so effectively. Yet it simultaneously allows an imaginative space for individual rendering. As form, this translates into an interesting and complex tension between the stock image and the fantasy of the creator.

There are two major chart publishing traditions presented here, each with its own personality. Broadly, they represent the north and south of India, one based in Delhi, and the other in Madurai, an old South Indian temple town.

Madurai is located close to Sivakasi, a small town which has the largest printing industry in India. Sivakasi printers offer the latest offset printing technology and the best prices, so the chart industry in Madurai relies a great deal on offset printing for its results. Madurai charts tend to be more painterly, with half-tone colour playing an important role in shaping images.

The Delhi chart industry is the older one, and the original art stems from letterpress technology, where images rendered in line art are later coloured in. However, more contemporary work is offset based, and less distinguishable from other chart art produced elsewhere.

While these are the two largest chart publishers, there are a number of smaller, more local ones which have their own distinctive styles of rendering.

On the whole, though, there is more which unites the various strands of chart publishing than distinguishes them. The majority of chart themes are common, with each publisher offering a minutely differing variation of the same thing. There is a lot of open borrowing, and it is not unusual to find several versions of the same chart in the same market. The question of copying does not arise here at all, since the understanding of origination in this context is very different. Indian popular art traditions do not clearly separate an authentic image from an ostensibly inauthentic 'version' or 'copy'. Every version is viewed as a variation on the original, somewhat like it, yet distinguishable from it.

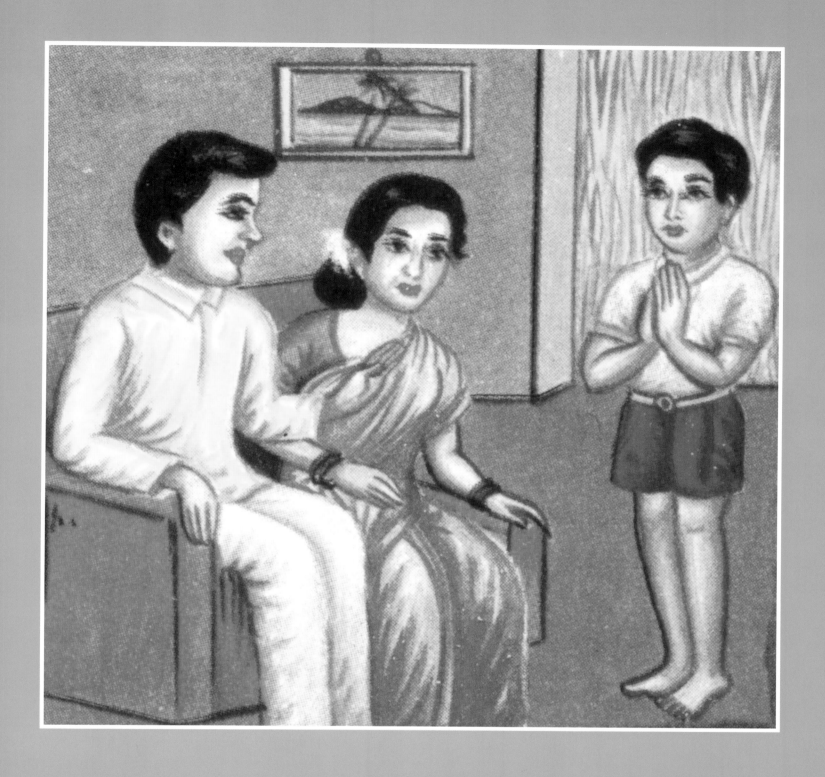

AN IDEAL BOY & BAD BEHAVIOUR

An Ideal Boy and Bad Behaviour

This set of vintage charts brilliantly captures the strong moral and didactic intent of Indian education. In many ways, it also holds the essence of the chart world – in both form and content.

Titles such as *Bad Habits* (p.18), *Human Stages and Duties* (p.20), *Cleanliness* (p.22) and *Rules of the Health Game* (p.26) directly instruct the individual on personal conduct. Bad behaviour is wide-ranging – eating fly infested food, taking the law into your own hands, flying kites on rooftops or playing cards all qualify. At the other end of the spectrum is *An Ideal Boy* (p.14). This frighteningly pious child has daily baths, salutes his parents in the morning, and takes lost children to the police station. It is hard to live by either code, but that is not really the point.

Other related charts deal with collective public and civic action, from community services to traffic rules and pollution control. Interestingly, they are not only about the realities of community life. They also hold up an ideal of civic order and the good society. *Community Cleanliness* (p.25), for example, has less to do with what exists than what ought to. In this sense they share a common ethical universe with the directly moral charts. This sort of chart does not strictly tell a story – each of its frames is a single instance, complete in itself.

Belonging to the same family are the moral stories. These are narrative sequences offering a clear story line with a moral. While some of them spell out their contents, many assume the reader to be familiar with the tale. So their sequences are generally purely visual, dispensing with a written story line, much like religious narrative panels that assume a pre-existing knowledge. Moral stories are an established form of literature in India, and some chart publishers also produce small storybooks to be read to children.

Moral stories originate from different sources, from the classical Indian fable collection *The Panchatantra*, to *Aesop's Fables*, the Buddhist *Jataka Tales*, and the Hindu epics *Ramayana* and *Mahabharatha*. Mythological comics are very popular in India and use the dramatic comic form to narrate legends and religious epics. But charts have limited space in which to tell their story. This constraint is especially well handled in *Mahabharatha* (p.40) which renders the longest epic in the world on a single page by skillfully highlighting well-known points of dramatic interest.

Unlike the more direct fable-based morals, the epic charts are not overtly didactic. They focus more tangentially on themes of familial love, fidelity, honour and wronged womanhood, all of which the child absorbs while filling in the gaps to complete the epic.

Hindu notions of duty and responsibility also construct *An Ideal Boy* which is, strictly speaking, part of the civic charts. Something interesting happens here though, as Hindu virtues meet another influence – a Christian ethic that links personal hygiene with moral worth.

The origins of this particular form of Christian ethic go back to the long history of missionary education in India. For the missionaries, one way of countering the evils of Indian society was through teaching proper values, clean habits and civic knowledge. This education would transform moral indifference and laxity into a recognition of right and wrong.

The charts also get their piety from a more contemporary source. The Indian government regularly circulates public messages of civic and moral intent: **Dowry – Bad to Receive, Bad to Give** or **One Man, One Tree** or even **Live Decent Family Life – Avoid Aids**. Found everywhere, the relationship of these sloganistic messages to policy or practice is tenuous, making them both habitual and gratuitous.

They echo the same abstract relationship that the chart messages have to their recipients. The disproportionately large number of charts on the theme of safety and first-aid, for example, would suggest a culture which lays great stress on civic alertness and safety. In reality, this is so far from practice as to be almost a fantasy. Like so much else, these exhortations become idealised information acquired for their own symbolic sake. Whatever the context, it seems unfair to expect a child to read *Bandages* (p.34) and bind a hernia victim in a complex 'double spica for groin'.

In the chart world, educated, urban, middle class people embody all the civic values worth emulating. *Safety First* (pp.32-33) takes this to a very practical level, going so far as to instruct the reader – more often than not, a working class child – not to live in a 'shaky house'. In *Community Cleanliness* a well-dressed urbanite helps to sweep the streets in a rural setting. Likewise, the ideal boy who helps lost children and delivers lectures to an admiring rural community is always already urban, educated and middle class. Unmarked by caste, an important determinant of status and identity in India, he lives in comfortable surroundings while he goes about his business.

The world-view of this set of charts incorporates all this. Some impulses are deliberate, others more submerged, yet they come together with a certain coherence. In artistic form, the influences are much more disparate and wide-ranging.

Cinema is an important stimulus. The depiction of the woman's condition in *Mahabharatha* and *Ramayana* (p.41) owes a lot to the body language of film heroines in the way they look coy and plead, or cringe with terror. In the *Moral Stories* (p.39), the thief (though not yet in prison) wears the striped T-shirt of the stage and screen prisoner. Tableaux of film sequences that celebrate the ideal family have obviously inspired *Family Members* (p.21). Backdrops also often resemble film sets, as in the *Mahabharatha* and *Ramayana*, where location is painted in using stock elements of interiors and exteriors. Sometimes the backdrop is purely a formal screen, as in the boy and banana peel sequence (p.19) where it does not impinge on the character and action, but remains insistently the same, like a cardboard film set.

Traditional influences are also present. In some cases, the art is reminiscent of folk traditions with flat colours and a visual hierarchy that does not reflect actual proportions. The size of an object signifies its importance in the narrative. This is so with the giant flat iron and human eye in *First Aid* (p.35), and in the panel 'eating unhygienic food' in *Bad Habits*, illustrated with flies the size of sparrows.

In other charts the traditional influence comes from religious paintings, with thick, lustrous drapery, ornamentation and well-defined, serene faces. *Municipal Community Service* (p.24), and *Community Cleanliness* are good examples. In *Human Stages and Duties*, the frame showing a baby with a ball replicates the countless pictures of the Hindu god Krishna as a baby, with a ball of butter in his hand (see also p.132).

Chart artists have access to old European art magazines for inspiration and many exteriors are rendered in a picturesque fashion, borrowing from sentimental western landscape paintings. Scenery with beautiful mountains and clean lakes are also used as backdrops, often primarily for aesthetic purposes. One of the moral stories (p.38) with a wonderful panel showing two cats and a monkey has curious echoes of medieval illuminated books.

The distinction between the Delhi and Madurai schools is most evident in this set of charts, when the two versions of *An Ideal Boy* are compared. The Delhi chart is more muted, tending to pale colours, and clean line art. The background is important and is rendered in some detail, with perspective achieved through proportion and line rather than colour.

Influenced a great deal by the bright and bold aesthetics of South Indian cinema, the Madurai chart favours strong block colours and flat, set-like backgrounds. It is the human character and his actions that stand out most.

Yet, despite the stylistic differences, both schools inhabit the same unmistakable moral world. They focus almost exclusively on the human condition, mixing what exists and what ought to. This tension between the stock image and artistic fantasy, is a dialogue which is central to the chart world.

AN IDEAL BOY - GOOD HABITS

GETS UP EARLY IN THE MORNING

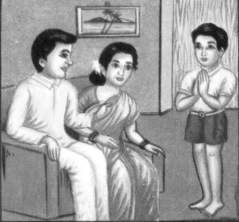

SALUTES PARENTS

GOES FOR MORNING WALK

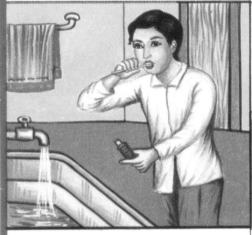

BRUSHES UP THE TEETH

BATHES DAILY

PRAYS

GOES TO SCHOOL AND READS ATTENTIVELY

TAKES MEALS IN TIME

HELPS OTHERS

TAKES PARTS IN GAMES

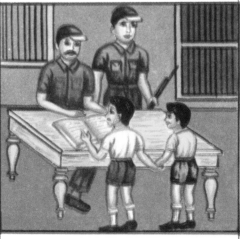

TAKING THE LOST CHILDREN TO THE POLICE POST

TAKES PART IN SOCIAL ACTIVITIES

14

AN IDEAL BOY
(GOOD HABITS)
आदर्श बालक

CHART NO. 1

सबेरे उठना ।
Gets up early in the morning.

माता-पिता को प्रणाम करना ।
Salutes parents.

सैर करना ।
Goes for Morning Walk.

दाँत साफ़ करना ।
Brushes up the teeth.

प्रति-दिन नहाना ।
Bathes daily.

प्रार्थना करना ।
PRAYS.

पाठशाला जाना व ध्यानपूर्वक पढ़ना ।
Goes to school & reads attentively.

समय पर भोजन करना ।
Takes meals in time.

दूसरों की सहायता करना ।
Helps others.

खेल-कूद में भाग लेना ।
Takes part in Games.

एन॰ सी॰ सी॰ से सम्बन्ध रखना ।
Joins N. C. C.

सामाजिक कार्यों में भाग लेना ।
Takes part in social activities.

BAD HABITS बुरी आदतें

THROWING LITTER IN OPEN OR STREETS
कूड़ा-करकट बाहर फेंकना

GAMBLING
जुआ खेलना

QUARRELLING
झगड़ा करना

ANIMAL-TEASING
जानवरों से छेड़-छाड़ करना

PLAYING WITH ELECTRICITY
बिजली से खेलना

PLAYING WITH TOOLS
औज़ारों से खेलना

KITE–FLYING OR PLAYING ON OPEN ROOFS
खुली छत पर खेलना व पतंग उड़ाना

PLAYING ON THE ROAD AND TRAVELLING ON FOOT BOARD
सड़क पर खेलना व बस में लटककर यात्रा करना

TO TAKE LAW IN HANDS
तोड़-फोड़ करना

USE OF IN HYGIENIC AND UNCLEAN EATABLES
खुली और गंदी चीजें खाना

STEALING
चोरी करना

PUB. BY : INDIAN BOOK DEPOT, 2937, BAHADUR GARH ROAD, NEAR DEPUTY GANJ, DELHI-6

Processing by BEST PHOTOLITHOGRAPHERS

Price: Rs. 1.00

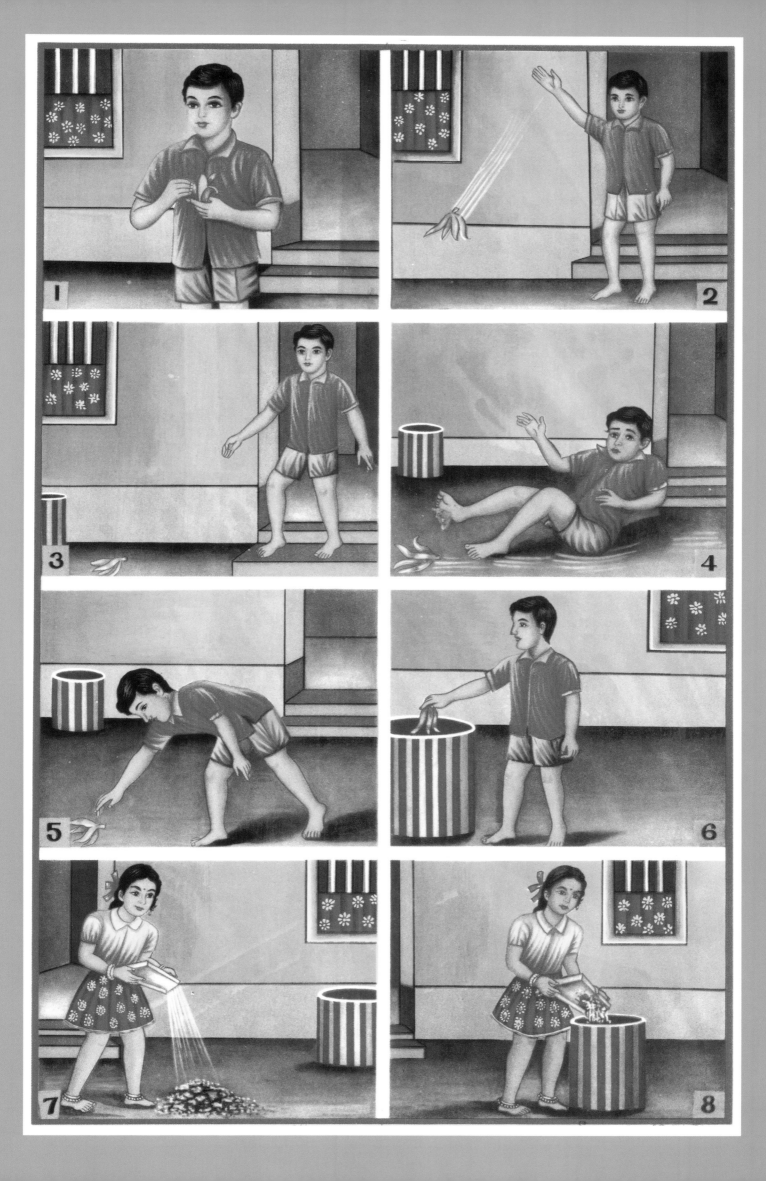

HUMAN STAGES AND DUTIES

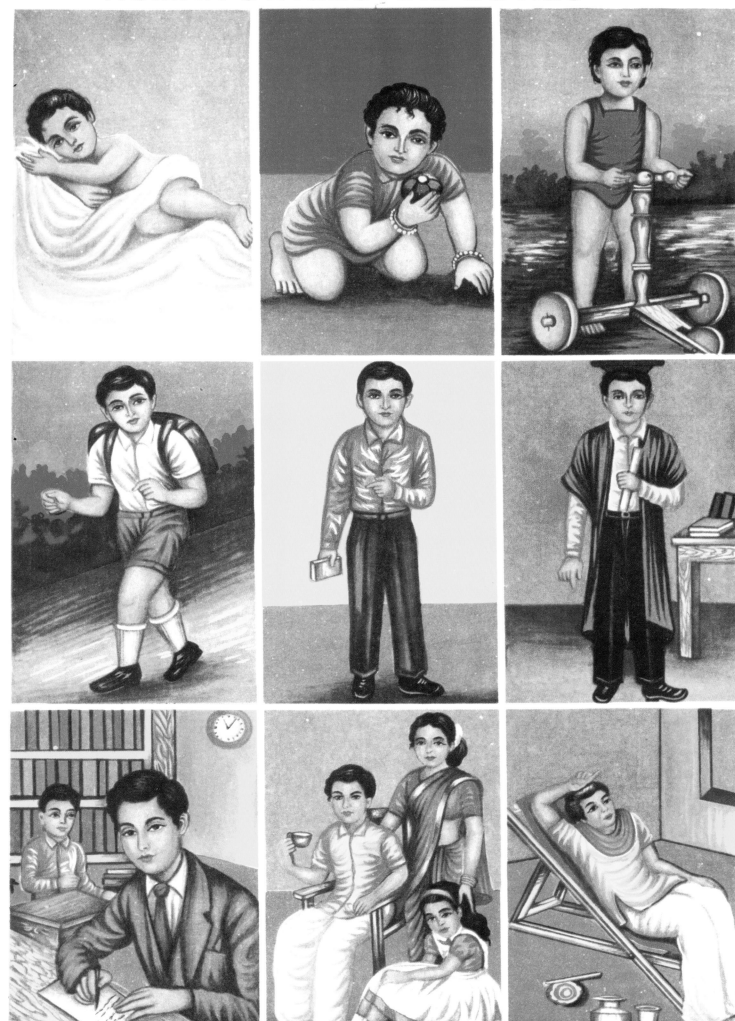

FAMILY MEMBERS
குடும்ப அங்கத்தினர்கள்

AN INDIVIDUAL FAMILY
தனிக்குடும்பம்

COMBINED FAMILY
கூட்டுக்குடும்பம்

21

INDIVIDUAL CLEANLINESS

VISIT THE LATRINE

BRUSH UP YOUR TEETH

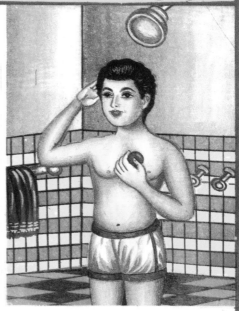

TAKE A BATH DAILY

CLEANESS YOUR HAIR

KEEP CLOTHES NEAT & CLEAN

TAKE MEALS IN TIME

GARGLE AFTER EVERY MEAL

KEEP HANDS & NAILS CLEAN

GO TO SCHOOL IN TIME

180

MUNICIPAL COMMITTEE SERVICE

VACCINATION

Hospital & Dispensaries

School

Road & Street lights

Libraries

Sanitation

Water Supply

Fire Brigade

House / Building Construction

24

COMMUNITY CLEANLINESS

CLEANING THE HOUSE

CLEANING THE VILLAGE

USE OF DUST - BINS

VILLAGE WELL BE KEPT NEAT & CLEAN

KEEP THE SCHOOL CLEAN

DESTROY MOSQUITOES TO AVOID DISEASES

DRAINAGE OF SULLAGE & SEWAGE INTO FIELD

KEEP THE VILLAGE LIBRARY NEAT & CLEAN

SRI RAM MADURAI

25

JUNIOR RED CROSS
RULES OF THE HEALTH GAME
जूनियर रेड क्रास
स्वास्थ्य के नियम

Be regular in going to latrine.
नियमानुसार सण्डास जाना ।

Clean your teeth properly every-day.
प्रति-दिन अच्छी तरह दाँत साफ़ करना ।

Take a bath everyday and dry your body with a clean cloth.
प्रतिदिन स्नान करना तथा शरीर को साफ़-सुथरे कपड़े से पूँछना ।

Keep your nails short and clean.
नाखुन छोटे व साफ़ रखना ।

Read in a good light.
अच्छी रोशनी में पढ़ना ।

Hold your body straight while standing.
खड़ा रहते समय शरीर को सीधा रखना ।

Do not spit on the ground.
फ़र्श पर न थूकना ।

कमरे में खाँसने या छींकने को टाल करना, तथा नाक साफ़ करने के लिए रूमाल प्रयोग करना ।

खाने के साथ पानी पीने की बजाय खाना खाने से आधा घण्टा पहले अथवा खाना खाने के एक घण्टा बाद बहुत सा स्वच्छ पानी पीना ।

Eat plenty of fresh fruits and vegetables. Chew your food well.
ताज़े फल व सब्ज़ियाँ खाना तथा खाना अच्छी तरह चबा कर खाना ।

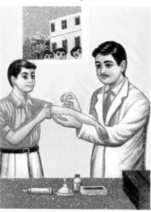

हर ३ साल के बाद तथा जब इलाके में चेचक फैली हो, चेचक का टीका लगवाना ।

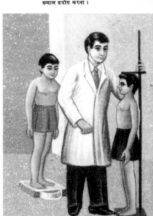

महीने में एक बार अपना तोल तथा साल में दो बार अपना नाप करवाना तथा उसका रिकार्ड रखना ।

Form queue habit.
पंक्ति में खड़े होने की आदत डालना ।

ऐसा खाना अथवा मिठाइयाँ जिन पर धूल पड़ी हो या मक्खियाँ बैठी हों, कभी भी न खाना ।

Play out of doors everyday and always breatne through the nose.
प्रतिदिन खुली हवा में खेलना तथा साँस केवल नाक द्वारा ही लेना ।

प्रतिदिन रात को खिड़कियाँ खोल कर तथा मुँह को ढके बिना 9 से 10 घण्टे तक सोना ।

Published by: Indian Book Depot, Map House . Bahadur Garh Road Delhi-6. Processing :- BEST PHOTO LITHO GRAPHERS

Price Re.1-00

26

POST & TELEGRAPH SERVICES

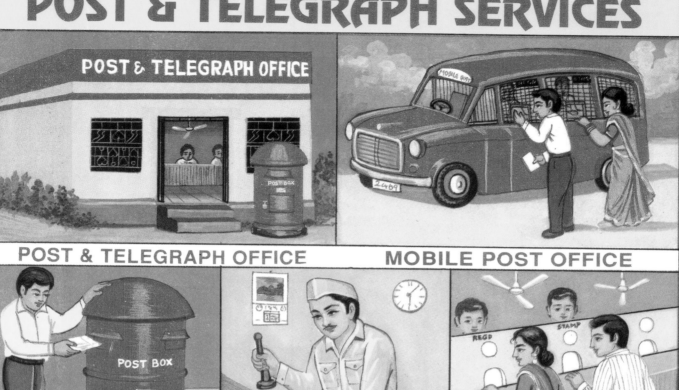

POST & TELEGRAPH OFFICE MOBILE POST OFFICE

POST BOX STAMPING THE LETTERS SALE OF POSTAL STAMPS & REGISTRATION

TELEPHONE SERVICE SAVINGS & MONEY ORDER SERVICES MEANS OF SENDING THE MAIL

TO SEND TELEGRAMS TO RECEIVE TELEGRAMS DELIVERY OF THE LETTERS

MAHESH ARTS·P.B. No: 42, SIVAKASI (INDIA)

POLLUTION & ENVIRONMENT CHART

Water should be protected from contamination.

Drains should be kept clean.

Throw litter into bins, keep the city clean.

Try to prevent mosquito breeding.

Vehicles should be regularly tune.

Always drink clean water

Excessive noise is harmful to human-ear.

There should be proper ventilation in the kitchen.

Whenever possible go on bicycle or walk.

Keep floors free from dust or dirt.

Wash vegetables/fruits before use.

Always use clean laterine.

Avoid smoking in confined spaces.

Avoid cutting of trees.

Drink clean water, while doing work.

Protection equipment should be kept with gases

Do not eat where chemicals are present

Try to control smoke emission.

Try to reduce road noise level.

Keep working premises clean.

28

Caused by

Prevented by

Contamination

filtering water

boiling water

drinking safe water

Walking barefoot

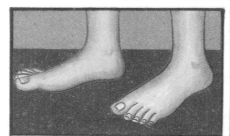

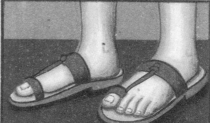

wearing footwear

Planting Farming

washing hands before eating and after using toilet

Covered with dust

Washing fruits and vegetables

through flies and insects

Controlling flies

29

TRAFFIC SIGNALS

THE VEHICLES COMING FROM BACK SIDE TO STOP

THE VEHICLES COMING FROM FRONT TO STOP

THE VEHICLES COMING FROM BOTH SIDES (Front back) TO STOP AT THE SAME TIME

THE VEHICLES COMING FROM FOUR SIDES (All Sides) TO STOP

THE VEHICLES COMING FROM LEFT SIDE TO PROCEED STRAIGHT FORWARD

THE VEHICLES COMING FORM RIGHT SIDE TO PROCEED STRAIGHT FORWARD

RULES TO FOLLOW

TRAFFIC LIGHTS

STOP

READY

GO

KEEP LEFT

WALK ON THE FOOT - PATH

RIGHT TURN	LEFT TURN	ZIG ZAG RIGHT	ZIG ZAG LEFT	SIDE ROAD RIGHT
SIDE ROAD LEFT	CROSS ROAD	MAJOR ROAD AHEAD	CUASE WAY ROAD	ROUGH ROAD
NARROW BRIDGE	PUBLIC BUS STOP	GO	NO PARKING	DO NOT TAKE "U" TURN

SPEED LIMIT 20 K.M.	RING ROAD	DEAD SLOW	SCHOOL	HUMP
END OF THE SPEED LIMIT AREA	USE OF SOUND HORN	CLOSED	NO OVERTAKING	LEVEL CROSSING GUARDED
STEEP HILL	ENTRY	NO ENTRY	DO NOT SOUND HORN	CHECK POST

ROAD TRAFFIC SIGNS

Rough Road

Zigzag Bend (Right)

Zigzag Bend (Left)

Steep Hill

Level Crossing (Guarded)

Right Turn

Left Turn

School

Parking

Over taking Prohibited

20
DEFINITION PLATE

CLOSED
Road Closed

Direction Sign

CLOSED TO
6 TONS

Always Follow These Rules

CROSS THE ROAD ONLY WHEN THE GREEN SIGNAL TELLS YOU TO CROSS.

1. WALK ON THE FOOT-PATH

ALWAYS STAND IN QUEUE AT THE BUS-STOP.

2. KEEP LEFT

1. Do'nt Throw Sweepings & Fruit-peels.

3. OBEY TRAFFIC SIGNALS

2. Do'nt Play, Jump & Loiter about on the Road.

4. Signal Clearly with your hand for taking a turn.

3. Walking & Passing through the heavy vehicles is dangerous.

5. Overtake only by the Right-hand side.

Ferry

Level Crossing

Side-Road (Left)

Narrow Bridge

Use of Sound Signals Prohibited

Speed Limit

Attention! Cross Roads

NO PARKING
No Parking

End of Speed Limit

DEAD SLOW

MAIN ROAD AHEAD

31

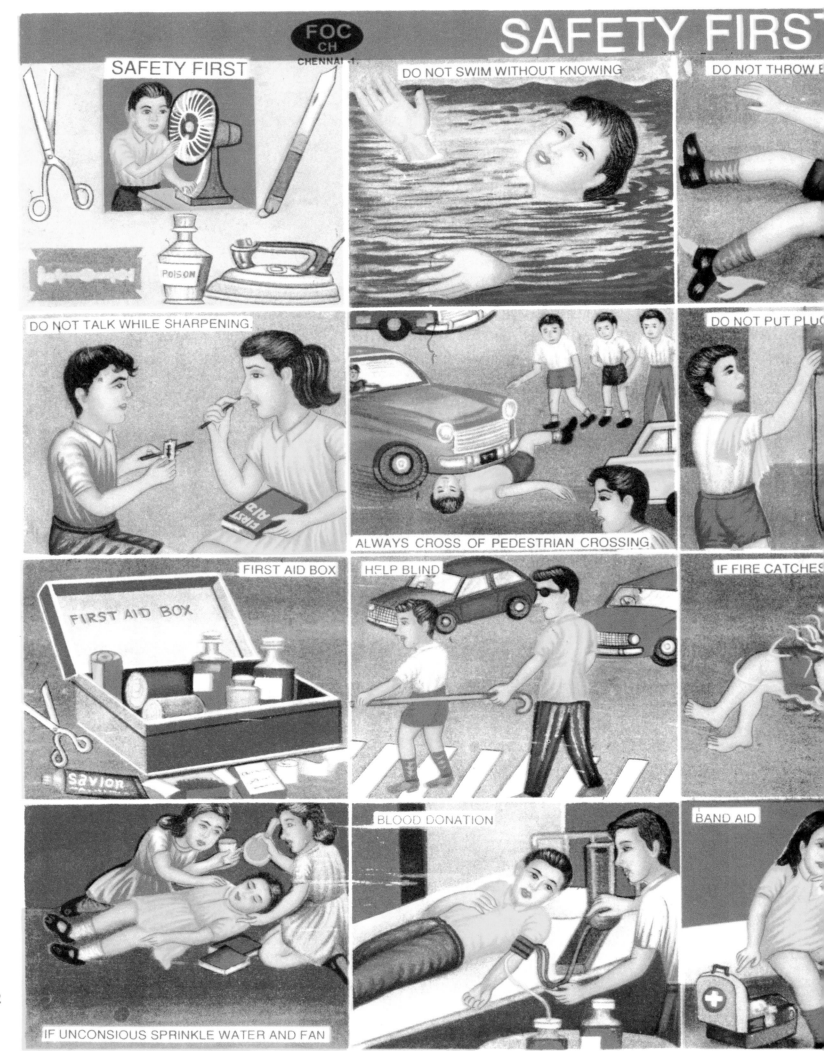

& FIRST AID

FIRST AID(BANDAGES)
प्राथमिक चिकित्सा (पट्टियाँ)

CHART No. 109

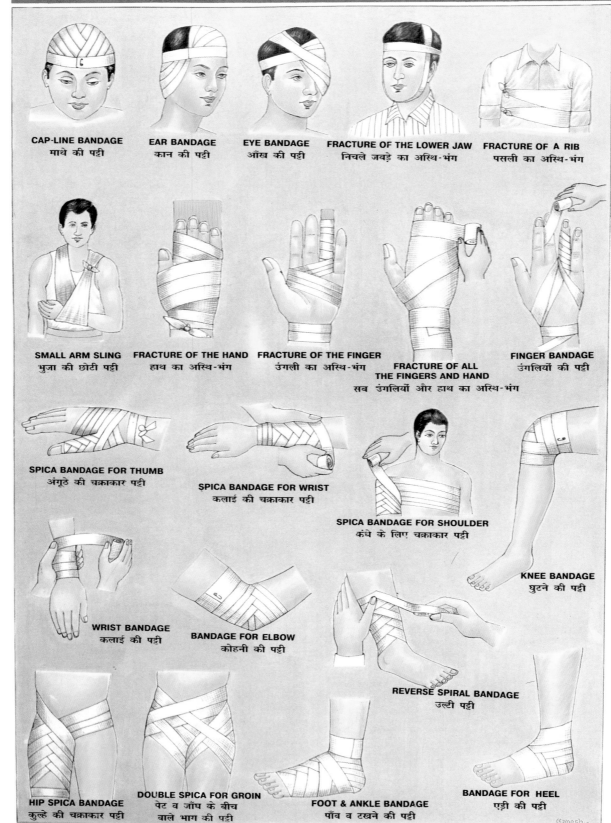

CAP-LINE BANDAGE
माथे की पट्टी

EAR BANDAGE
कान की पट्टी

EYE BANDAGE
आँख की पट्टी

FRACTURE OF THE LOWER JAW
निचले जबड़े का अस्थि-भंग

FRACTURE OF A RIB
पसली का अस्थि-भंग

SMALL ARM SLING
भुजा की छोटी पट्टी

FRACTURE OF THE HAND
हाथ का अस्थि-भंग

FRACTURE OF THE FINGER
उंगली का अस्थि-भंग

FRACTURE OF ALL THE FINGERS AND HAND
सब उंगलियों और हाथ का अस्थि-भंग

FINGER BANDAGE
उंगलियों की पट्टी

SPICA BANDAGE FOR THUMB
अंगूठे की चक्राकार पट्टी

SPICA BANDAGE FOR WRIST
कलाई की चक्राकार पट्टी

SPICA BANDAGE FOR SHOULDER
कंधे के लिए चक्राकार पट्टी

KNEE BANDAGE
घुटने की पट्टी

WRIST BANDAGE
कलाई की पट्टी

BANDAGE FOR ELBOW
कोहनी की पट्टी

REVERSE SPIRAL BANDAGE
उल्टी पट्टी

HIP SPICA BANDAGE
कुल्हे की चक्राकार पट्टी

DOUBLE SPICA FOR GROIN
पेट व जाँघ के बीच वाले भाग की पट्टी

FOOT & ANKLE BANDAGE
पाँव व टखने की पट्टी

BANDAGE FOR HEEL
एड़ी की पट्टी

PUBLISHED BY : **INDIAN BOOK DEPOT (MAP HOUSE)**, 2937, Bahadur Garb Road, Near Deputy Ganj. Delhi-6.   Price Rs.: 2.00

PROCESSING BY : TOP OFFSET LITHOGRAPHERS, 3277563, 3260672   Printed by : Shalini Offset Press.

34

FIRST AID

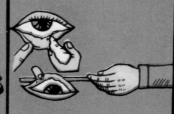
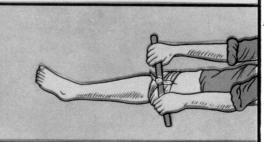

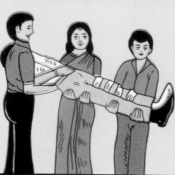

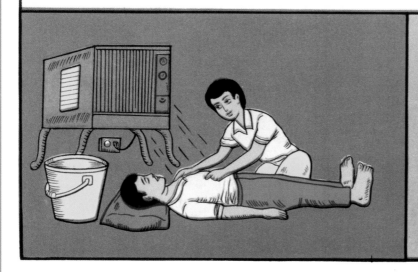
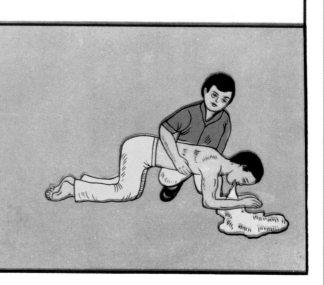

THE LION AND THE MOUSE

The mouse ran over the lion. Lion caught the mouse.

The mouse said, "Please don't eat me, I will help you."

The lion left the mouse and went away.

One day the lion was caught inside the hunters net. He roard aloud.

The mouse heard the roar, it ran to help the lion. It cut the net into pieces.

The lion came out of the net. He thanked the mouse.

MORAL :- "DO NOT UNDER ESTIMATE BY LOOK"

SRI RAM Madurai - 1. PHONE : 733982, 736331

MORAL STORIES

Slow, & Steady wins the race.

"Grapes are Sour" Do'nt try to do anything which is beyond your reach.

As you sow, so shall you reap.

Do'nt give way to flattery.

MORAL STORIES

THE FAITHFUL DOG

A man had a Pet dog. One night a thief broke into house and dog began to bark.

Master got up, finding nobody in the house he started beating the dog.

After sometime the thief again broke into the house. The dog saw him burrying valueable under the tree

The dog led his master to the same tree and dug the ornaments. The master was happy.

YOU CAN NEVER PLEASE EVERY ONE

A father and son were going to sell their ass. people said, "You have your own ass and you are walking"

Father told his son to ride on. A brahmin said to son that your father is walking and you are riding.

Then father also rode on. A villager said cruels your ass is dying with your weight.

They tied the legs of the ass with bamboo and carried on shoulder. On the bridge the people made noise. The ass took fright and fell down in the river.

UNITED WESTAND DIVIDED WE FALL

An old sick man had four sons, they always quarrelled with each other. He wanted to give them last lesson.

He asked his sons to bring some sticks to break. Each son broke the stick easily.

Then he gave them a bundle to break but none of them could break.

At last the old man adviced that union is strength.

TWO CATS AND THE MONKEY

Two cats stole a piece of cheese and started quarrelling for their shares.

They went to a monkey for justice.

Monkey made two uneven pieces and started weighing. He started eating a big piece from the lower side of the scales

Monkey ate the remaining piece saying "This is for my services" Cats lost everything

MORAL STORIES CHART
NO.4
CHART NO. 119

The Faith ful Dog.　　　　　　　　　　　　स्वाभिभक्त कुत्ता।

Those who try to please all sure to please none.　　सब को प्रसन्न नहीं किया जा सकता।

Union is strength.　　　　　　　　　　　　एकता में बल है।

Two Cats & The Monkey.　　　　　　　दो बिल्लियाँ और बन्दर।

Artwork by : Sapna Advertising

39

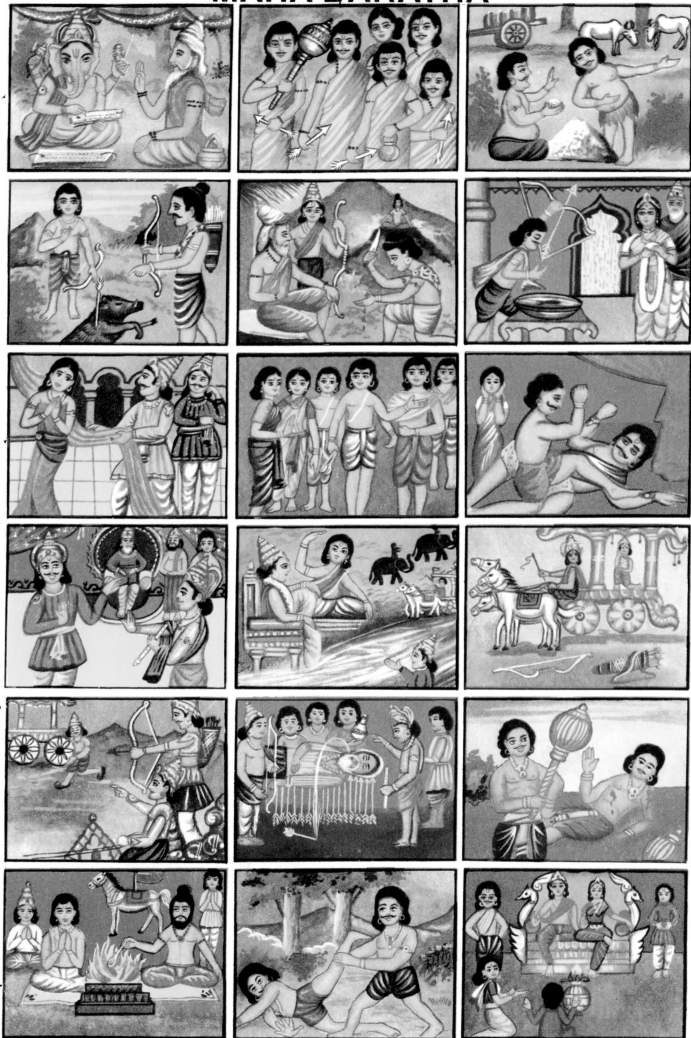

40

RAMAYANA

Sri Ram Madurai

SRI RAM Madurai - 1.   PHONE : 733982, 736331

NO. 89

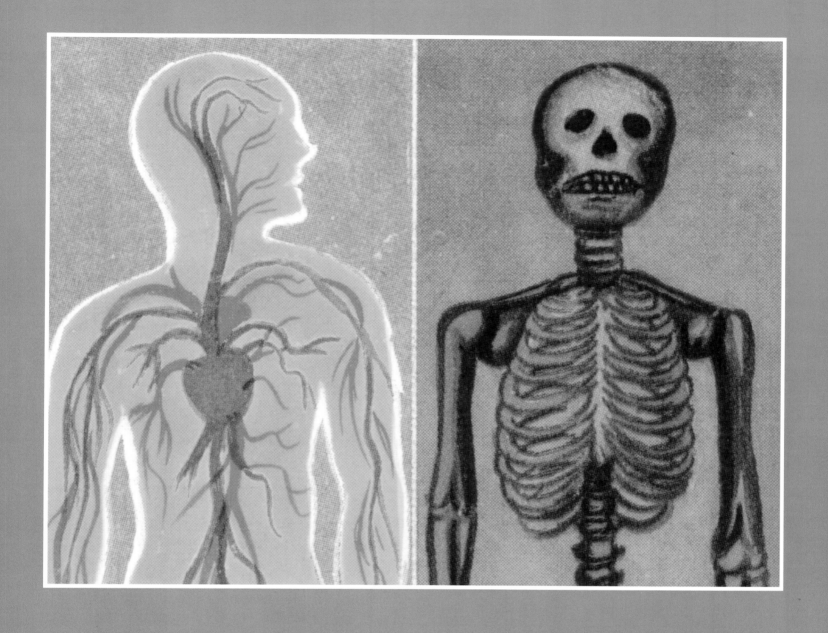

LIVING &
NON-LIVING ARTICLES

Living and Non-Living Articles

A large number of charts are devoted to the scientific spirit in one way or another. This is a broad category, from charts that deal with recognisable topics in science to ones that take on the staggering range of Living and Non-living Articles.

In the more general charts – *Useful Articles* (p.46), *School Articles* (p.47), or *Home Science* (p.50) – the aim is not so much scientific observation, as a classification and labeling of the familiar. Technology features here as well, sometimes in the form of home appliances, other times as means of transport. The fusion of these separate themes under one heading reflects the looseness with which charts themselves approach categories.

While the science charts are completely charming, there is also a poignancy to them. The earnest students who use them have few other sources of information apart from their textbooks. Seen critically, the most careless of the charts could actually damage the understanding of the student by disregarding both facts and the rational structure that the study of science requires. Though textbooks are not as cavalier as this, these charts do capture something larger about the state of mass science education in India.

In Sources of *Water and Shadows* (p.64), the reader is forced to consider – simultaneously – two phenomena that do not have a common source. Likewise, a panel on frogs and another on hens has been included in *Developmental Stages of Insects* (p.58). Spelling mistakes are present here, as in many other charts, but are highlighted all the more in this set because of their importance in making sense of content. 'Pulcuram' replaces fulcrum, for instance, or a young frog becomes a 'tadbole' in a phonetic guess. The relationship between label and image is also curious. In *Sources of Water and Shadows*, the shadows themselves are missing from the panels. It is as if the very labeling of something places the object adequately for the viewer. The image represents an already self-evident fact.

By and large, science is less a way of enquiry than a baroque collection of information. The beautifully painted birds chart (p.57) captures this exactly. It seems a reasonable enough theme – until the viewer notices the choice of rare birds and that the beaks, claws and eggs shown in the same row do not belong to the same bird. It is fairly certain that most Indian children will never get to see the beak of a Montezumaor Penola, the claw of a Purple Gallinule or the egg of a Bennet's Cassowary.

The unimportance of context is also evident in *Seasons* (pp.66-67). Only two of the four panels – Rainy Season and Hot Season – are true for most of India. Clearly borrowed from western references, neither the clothing nor most of the activities suggested have anything to do with local reality.

In form, this set of charts is possibly the most painstakingly rendered, with great attention to colour, shape and tone. A majority of the scientific charts are influenced by images from text and reference books. But unlike the originals, the artist is not concerned with scientific accuracy or anatomical precision so much as a great care in rendering. The images stand in for – rather than faithfully reproduce – their subjects. Each panel appears more like a painting, carefully shaded and highlighted, as if the point of the drawing was not to capture the subject as it is, but to tease it out into a form that represents it better, and more ideally, than a faithful representation would. Where the form works beautifully is in the simpler charts for younger children. In *Vegetables* (p.55), for example, the individual glow of each vegetable brings out its character and enhances its allure more than a purely realistic rendering could.

The botanical charts are reminiscent of drawings of exotic plants and flowers by early nineteenth century English naturalists. But in the flowers chart (p.56), the artist favours aesthetic sensibility over botanical detail, to convey a general authenticity of feeling. It is in charts like *Human Anatomy* (p.51), that demand accuracy and detail, that this becomes a problem. Here the grid follows the convention of early medical oleographs, but the rendering is more concerned with narrative and expression, more like a public awareness message than an anatomical diagram.

Precision and empirical fidelity are not the prime concerns of the science charts. Where the subject matter requires neither, they perform their task brilliantly. In all other cases, though enjoyable, their educational value is suspect. But perhaps there is different way of looking at it. Instead of illustrating observable data or reasoned arguments, the artists may be giving form to another impulse altogether: the unique aura that science enjoys in India. The reverential *Inventors and Scientists* (p.73) is a good example of the chart artist's understanding of this mystique. Science is a force in its own right, with all the power of a modern, rational enterprise. It exists almost as a religion, and the science charts, like religious lithographs that take on a sacral quality, seem to possess a powerful and self-evident value.

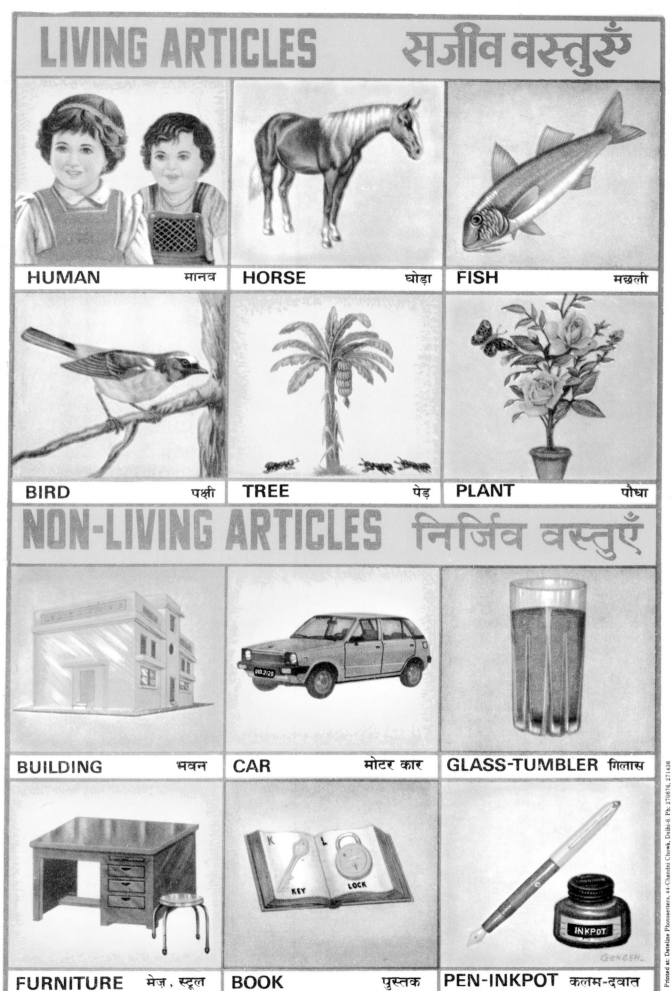

LIVING ARTICLES सजीव वस्तुएँ

HUMAN मानव	HORSE घोड़ा	FISH मछली
BIRD पक्षी	TREE पेड़	PLANT पौधा

NON-LIVING ARTICLES निर्जीव वस्तुएँ

BUILDING भवन	CAR मोटर कार	GLASS-TUMBLER गिलास
FURNITURE मेज़, स्टूल	BOOK पुस्तक	PEN-INKPOT कलम-दवात

PUBLISHED BY: INDIAN BOOK DEPOT. MAP HOUSE, BAHADUR GARH ROAD, DELHI-6   Rs. 1.00

Printed at: Dateline Photosetters, 44-Chandni Chowk, Delhi-6 Ph: 270676, 271436

USEFUL ARTICLES

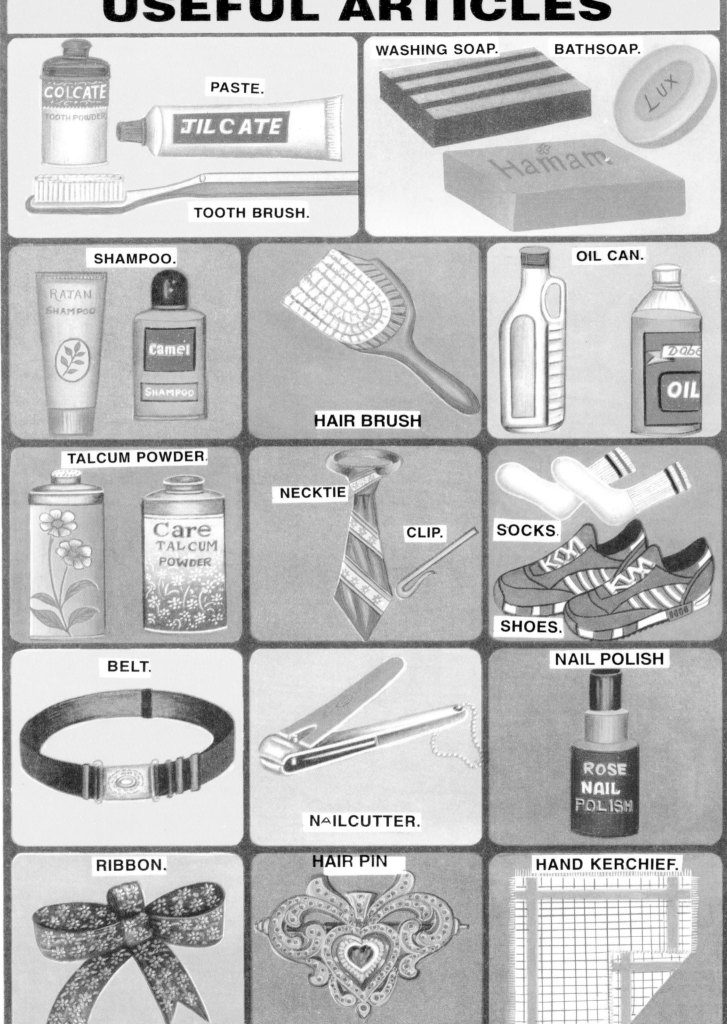

PASTE.

COLGATE TOOTH POWDER

JILCATE

TOOTH BRUSH.

WASHING SOAP.   BATHSOAP.

Lux

Hamam

SHAMPOO.

RATAN SHAMPOO

camel SHAMPOO

HAIR BRUSH

OIL CAN.

OIL

TALCUM POWDER.

Care TALCUM POWDER

NECKTIE

CLIP.

SOCKS.

SHOES.

BELT.

NAILCUTTER.

NAIL POLISH

ROSE NAIL POLISH

RIBBON.

HAIR PIN

HAND KERCHIEF.

46

SCHOOL ARTICLES

47

SRI RAM MADURAI.

आकृतियाँ SHAPES

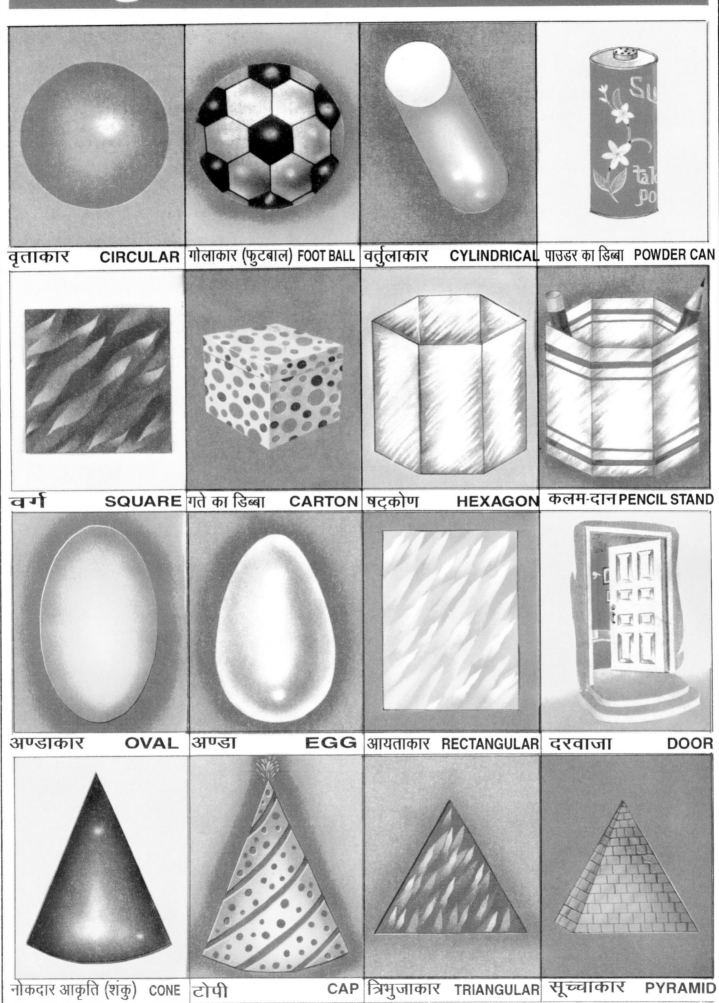

वृत्ताकार **CIRCULAR**	गोलाकार (फुटबाल) **FOOT BALL**
वर्तुलाकार **CYLINDRICAL**	पाउडर का डिब्बा **POWDER CAN**
वर्ग **SQUARE**	गत्ते का डिब्बा **CARTON**
षट्कोण **HEXAGON**	कलम-दान **PENCIL STAND**
अण्डाकार **OVAL**	अण्डा **EGG**
आयताकार **RECTANGULAR**	दरवाजा **DOOR**
नोकदार आकृति (शंकु) **CONE**	टोपी **CAP**
त्रिभुजाकार **TRIANGULAR**	सूच्चाकार **PYRAMID**

48

DIFFERENT TYPES OF HOUSES

PERMANENT

MOVABLE

MOBILE

FLAT ROOF

SLOPING ROOF

SEMI-CIRCULAR ROOF

PALMLEAF ROOF

TIN ROOF

CEMENT ROOF

TILED ROOF

STRAW ROOF

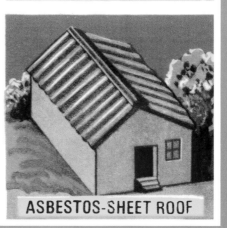

ASBESTOS-SHEET ROOF

HOME SCIENCE — COOKING & UTENSILS CHART

Chart No. 45

HUMAN ANATOMY

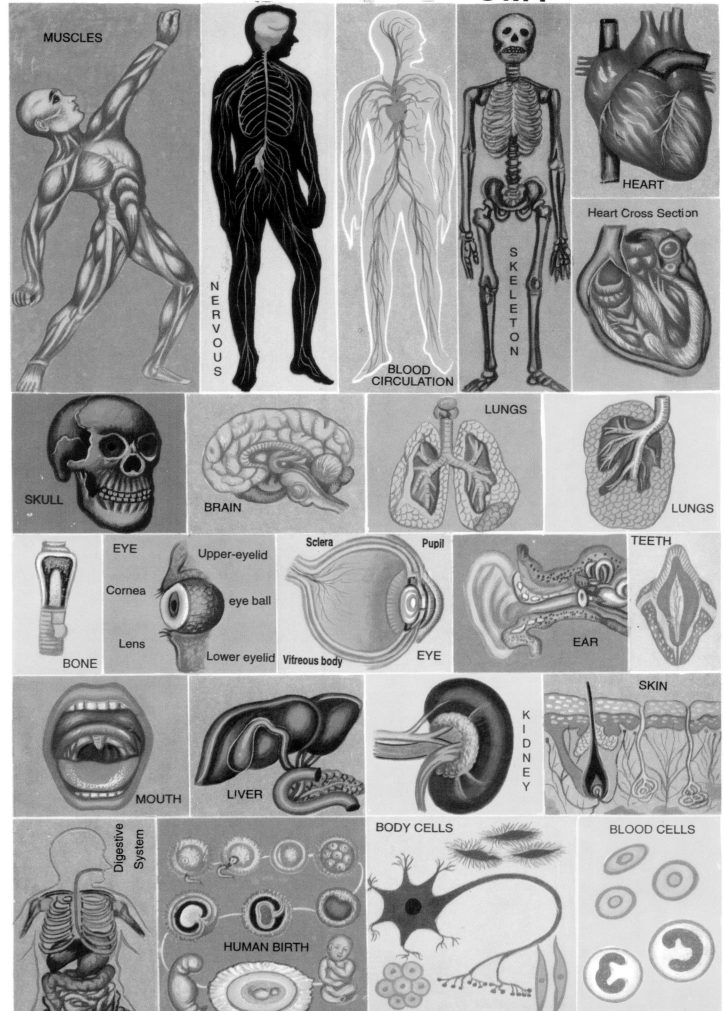

MUSCLES

NERVOUS

BLOOD CIRCULATION

SKELETON

HEART

Heart Cross Section

SKULL

BRAIN

LUNGS

LUNGS

BONE

EYE
Upper-eyelid
Cornea
eye ball
Lens
Lower eyelid

Sclera
Pupil
Vitreous body
EYE

EAR

TEETH

MOUTH

LIVER

KIDNEY

SKIN

Digestive System

HUMAN BIRTH

BODY CELLS

BLOOD CELLS

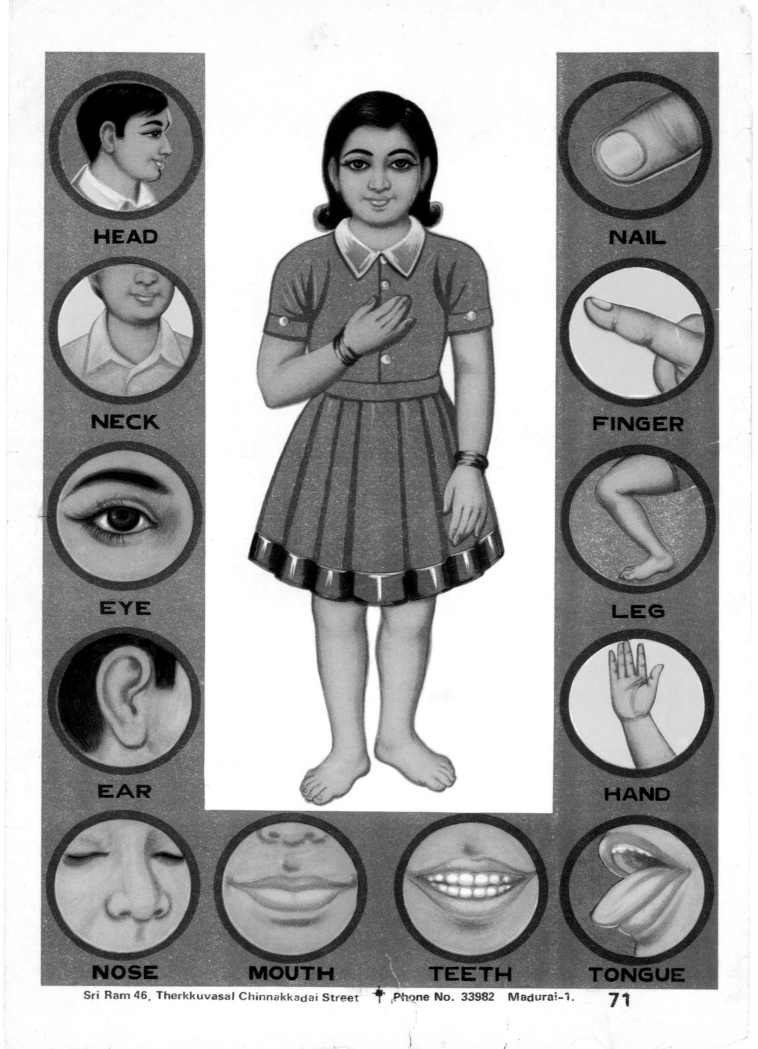

HEAD

NECK

EYE

EAR

NAIL

FINGER

LEG

HAND

NOSE

MOUTH

TEETH

TONGUE

52

Sri Ram 46, Therkkuvasal Chinnakkadai Street   Phone No. 33982   Madurai-1.   71

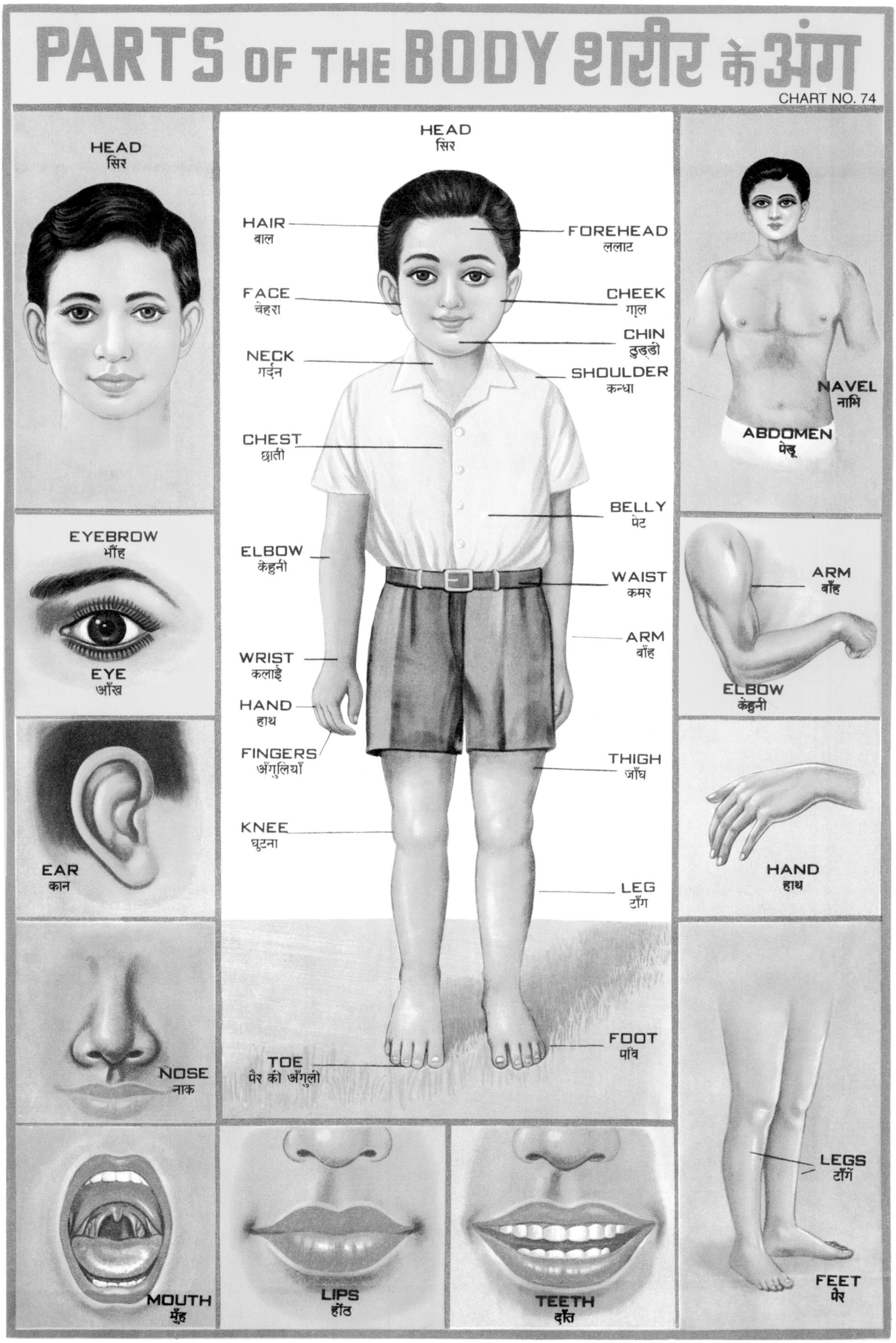

PARTS OF THE BODY शरीर के अंग

HEAD
सिर

HEAD
सिर

HAIR
बाल

FOREHEAD
ललाट

FACE
चेहरा

CHEEK
गाल

CHIN
ठुड्डी

NECK
गर्दन

SHOULDER
कन्धा

CHEST
छाती

BELLY
पेट

ELBOW
केहुनी

WAIST
कमर

ARM
बाँह

WRIST
कलाई

HAND
हाथ

FINGERS
अँगुलियाँ

THIGH
जाँघ

KNEE
घुटना

LEG
टाँग

EYEBROW
भौंह

EYE
आँख

EAR
कान

NOSE
नाक

FOOT
पाँव

TOE
पैर की अँगुली

NAVEL
नाभि

ABDOMEN
पेड़ू

ARM
बाँह

ELBOW
केहुनी

HAND
हाथ

LEGS
टाँगें

MOUTH
मुँह

LIPS
होंठ

TEETH
दाँत

FEET
पैर

53

LEAVES

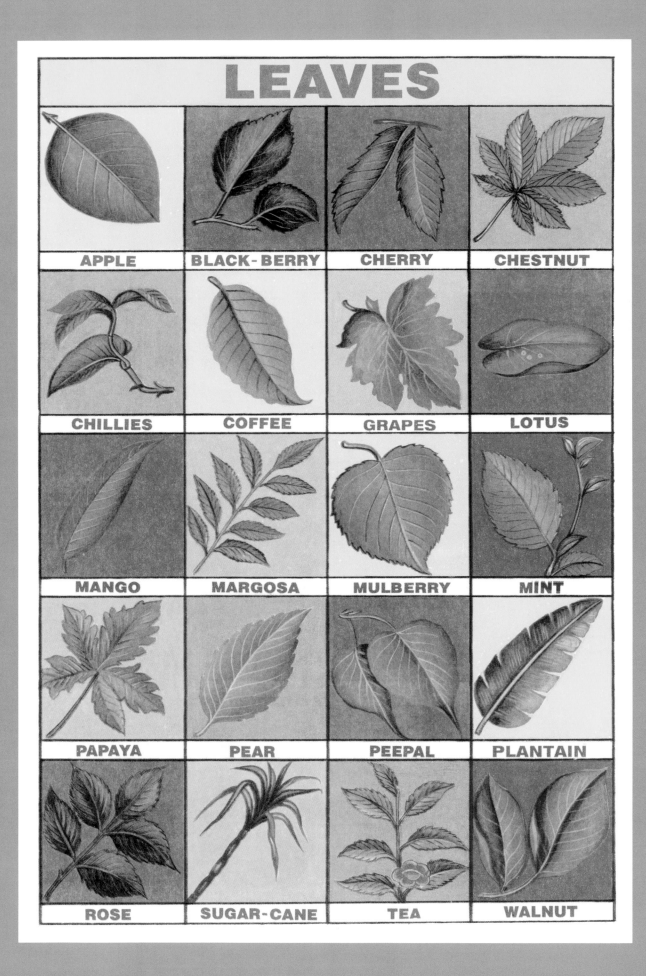

APPLE · BLACK-BERRY · CHERRY · CHESTNUT

CHILLIES · COFFEE · GRAPES · LOTUS

MANGO · MARGOSA · MULBERRY · MINT

PAPAYA · PEAR · PEEPAL · PLANTAIN

ROSE · SUGAR-CANE · TEA · WALNUT

54

VEGETABLES

POMEIO

JIMIKAND
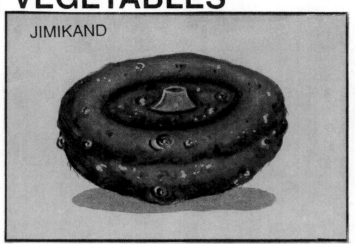

ESCULENTE - ROOT

BREAD FRUIT
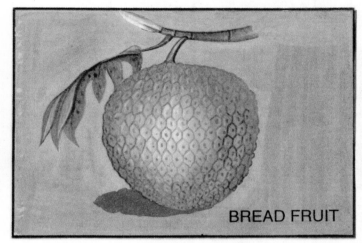

LEMON

GINGER

STAR FRUIT

RADISH
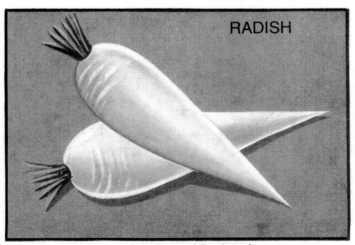

No 5 Sri Ram Madurai

WATER LILLY

ASOKU

MARIGOLD

JASMINE

BLUE BELL

GARDEN LILLY

DAHLIA

CORN FLOWER

1

Sri Ram Madurai

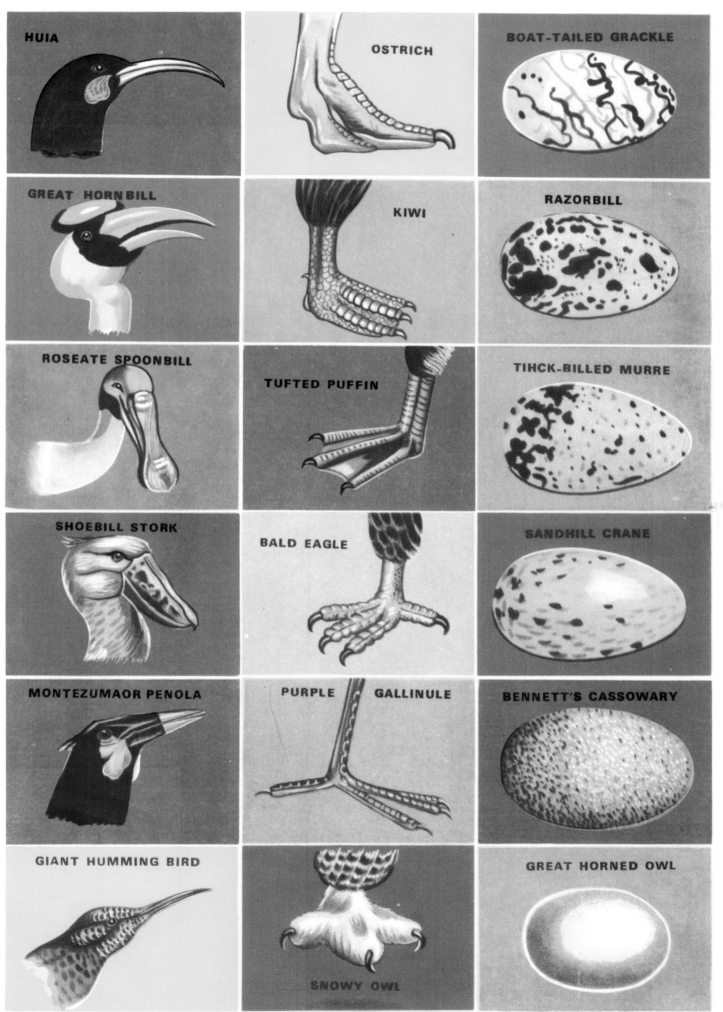

HUIA

OSTRICH

BOAT-TAILED GRACKLE

GREAT HORNBILL

KIWI

RAZORBILL

ROSEATE SPOONBILL

TUFTED PUFFIN

TIHCK-BILLED MURRE

SHOEBILL STORK

BALD EAGLE

SANDHILL CRANE

MONTEZUMAOR PENOLA

PURPLE GALLINULE

BENNETT'S CASSOWARY

GIANT HUMMING BIRD

SNOWY OWL

GREAT HORNED OWL

Sri Ram Madurai

57

79

DEVELOPMENTAL STAGES OF INSECTS

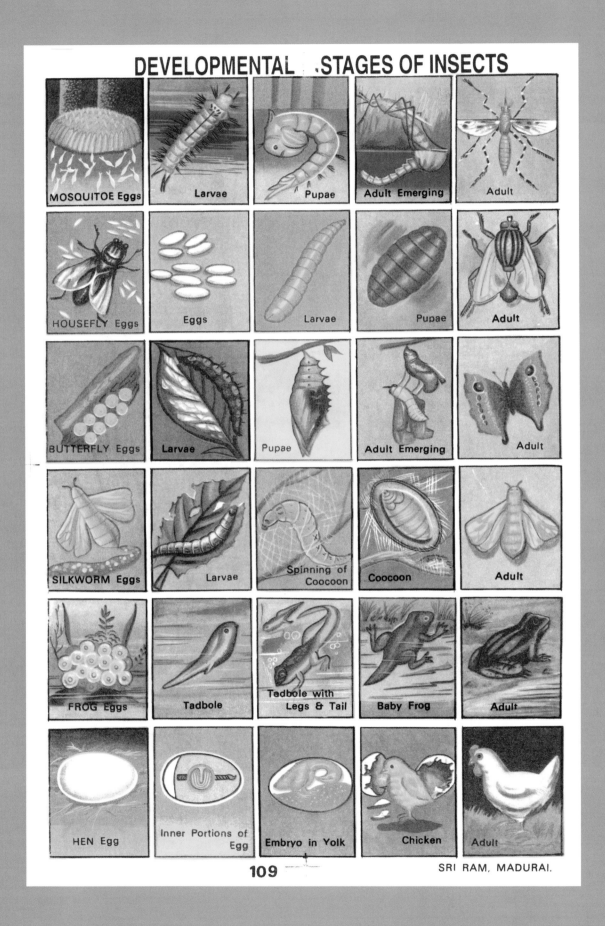

MOSQUITOE Eggs	Larvae	Pupae	Adult Emerging	Adult
HOUSEFLY Eggs	Eggs	Larvae	Pupae	Adult
BUTTERFLY Eggs	Larvae	Pupae	Adult Emerging	Adult
SILKWORM Eggs	Larvae	Spinning of Coocoon	Coocoon	Adult
FROG Eggs	Tadbole	Tadbole with Legs & Tail	Baby Frog	Adult
HEN Egg	Inner Portions of Egg	Embryo in Yolk	Chicken	Adult

ANIMALS & THEIR EATABLES

LION   TIGER   FOX

COW   GOAT   DONKEY

ELEPHANT   CAT   GIRAFFE

CAMEL   RABBIT   SNAKE

No. 232   SRI RAM Madurai - 1. PHONE : 733982, 736331.

EARLY MAN
आदि मानव

The time span of huma
to the present shape o

The near men.

Early Men caught small animals to eat, using stones to kill their preys.

About 3,5
people firs
make fire.

Early Men worked together to hunt big animals.

Early Men made clothes from animal skins.

Various typ
made by Ea

...ution (beginning from ape
... is about 25 million years.

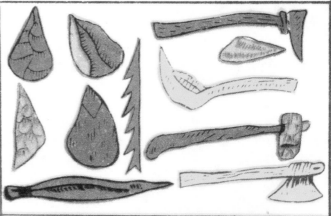

Some of the weapons/tools
of Stone Age.

... years ago,
...ned how to

Early Men cooking meat
on the fire.

Early Man making stone tools.

...huts/houses
...en.

Huts were made out of
wood near rivers.

Farming was slowly developed.
Animals came to be tendered up.

61

STONE AGE

PRIMITIVE MAN

SKIN DRESS

CLOTHES OF GRASSES

HUNTING

FISHING

MAKING FIRE WITH STONES

SHELTER OF SKINS

HOUSE OF STONE

HOUSE OF STRAW

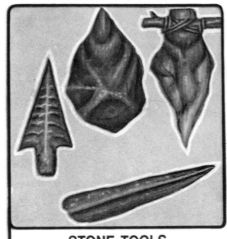

STONE TOOLS

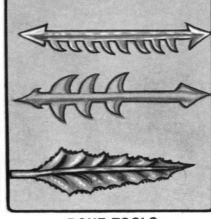

BONE TOOLS

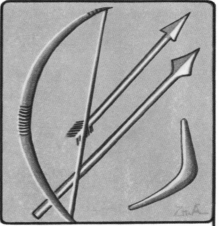

SPEAR & ARROW

62

UNIVERSAL CREATIONS

SUN

MOUNTAIN

VOLCANO

RIVER

RAINBOW

129

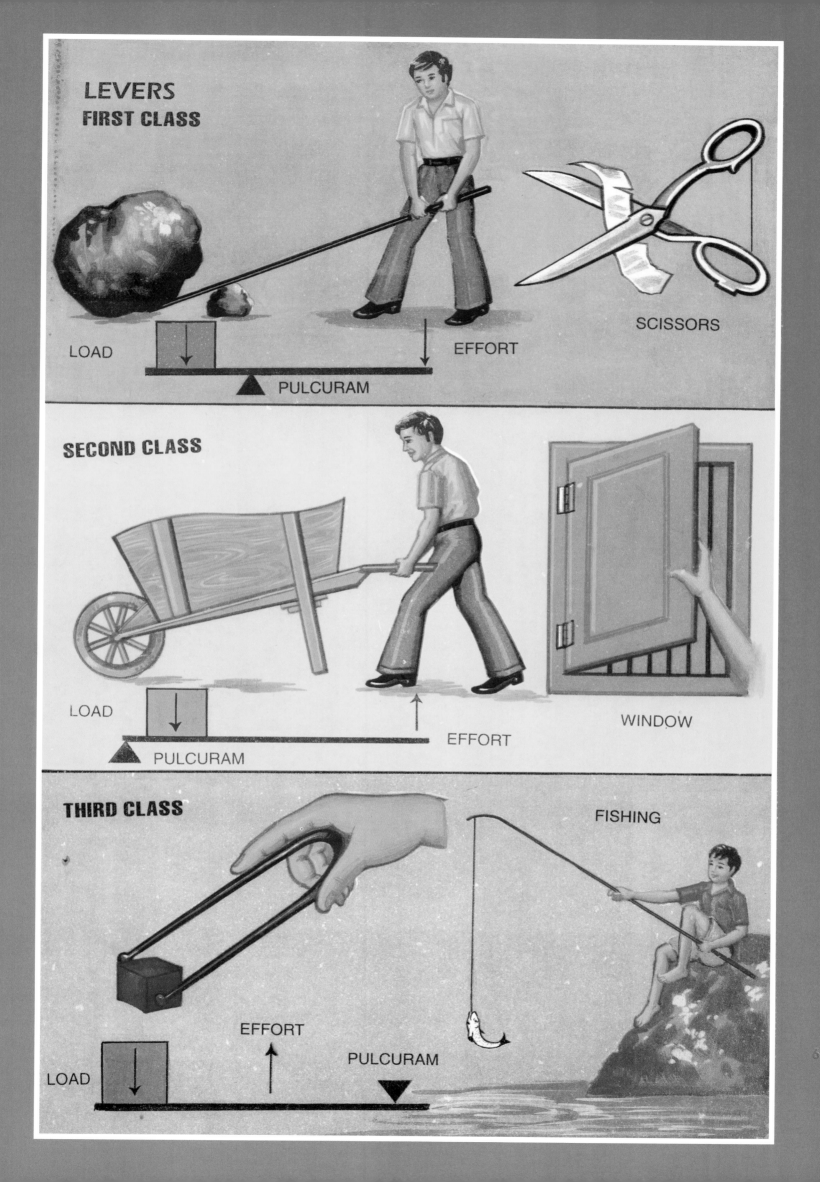

LEVERS
FIRST CLASS

LOAD

PULCURAM

EFFORT

SCISSORS

SECOND CLASS

LOAD

PULCURAM

EFFORT

WINDOW

THIRD CLASS

FISHING

LOAD

EFFORT

PULCURAM

65

SEASONAL WEAR

RAINY SEASON

HOT SEASON

AUTUMN

COLD WINTER

66

ONS

67

CAMERA

TELESCOPE

MICROSCOPE

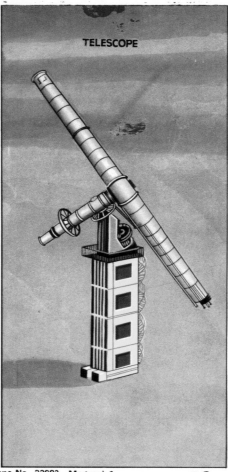
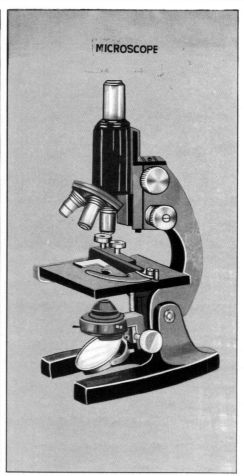

6 2

IMPROVEMENT OF THE COOKING - STOVE FROM THE ANCIENT DAYS

ANCIENT FIRE WOOD BURNER

MUD POTTERY FIRE WOOD BURNER

STEEL PLATE STOVE FOR COAL BURNER

TANK BASED BLOW STOVE

SEPARATE TANK BLOW STOVE

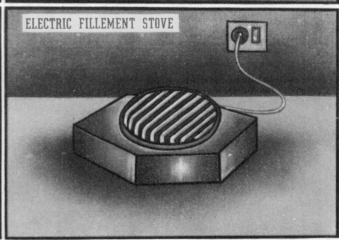

ELECTRIC FILLEMENT STOVE

PETROLIUM GAS STOVE

WICK STOVE FOR KEROSENE

MEANS OF COMMUNICATION

TELEPHONE   RADIO TAPE RECORDER   TELEVISION   VIDEO RECORDE

  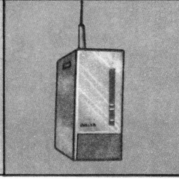 

RECORD PLAYAR   TELEPRINTER (TELEX)   WALKIE TALKIE   MICROPHONE

SATELLITE   CINEMA PROJECTER   FAX   NEWS PAPER

   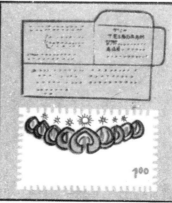

CORRESPONDENCE   SIGNAL   COMPUTER   POST & TELEGRAPH

70

SRI RAM MADURAI   No:160

MEANS OF TRANSPORT

CYCLE

CYCLE RICKSHAW

TONGA

BULLOCK CART

CAMEL CART

MOTOR RICKSHAW

AUTO RICKSHAW

BUS

MOTOR CAR

TRACTOR

JEEP

SCOOTER, MOTOR CYCLE

TRUCK, TEMPO

DOUBLE DECKER BUS

ELECTRIC TRAIN

BOAT

SHIP

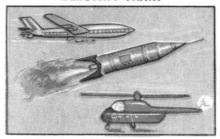
AEROPLANE, HELICOPTOR, ROCKET

71

96

Sri Ram Madurai

BYCYCLE

MOTOR BOAT

TRACTOR

ELECTRIC TRAIN

SHIP

SCOOTER

AEROPLANE

Sri Ram Madurai

45

INVENTORS & SCIENTISTS
आविष्कारक तथा वैज्ञानिक

CHART NO. 51

LAW OF PHOTOELECTRIC EFFECT (ATOM)

THEORY OF EVOLUTION

TELEPHONE

ALBERT EINSTEIN एलबर्ट आइन्स्टाईन   **ROBERT CHARLES DARWIN** रॉबर्ट चार्ल्स डार्विन   **ALEXANDER GRAHAM BELL** एलैक्जन्डर ग्रॅहम बेल

NUCLEAR SCIENCE

CRYSTAL DYNAMICS

LIGHTNING CONDUCTOR

DR. HOMI J. BHABHA डॉ. एच.जे. भाभा   **DR. C.V. RAMAN** डॉ. सी.वी. रामन   **BENJAMIN FRANKLIN** बेंजामिन फ्रंकलीन

AEROPLANE

CIRCULATION OF BLOOD

LAW OF GRAVITATION & MOTION

WILBUR WRIGHT विल्बर राईट   **WILLIAM HARVEY** विलियम हार्वे   **SIR ISAAC NEWTON** सर इसाक न्यूटन

DYNAMITE

STEAM ENGINE

LAW OF FLOTATION

ALFRED NOBLE अल्फ्रेड नोबल   **JAMES WATT** जेम्स वॉट्   **ARCHIMEDES** आर्कीमिडीज,

TELEVISION

INCANDESCENT BULB

ROCKET

J.L. BAIRD जे. एल. बेयर्ड   **THOMAS ALVA EDISON** थॉम्स अल्वा एडिसन   **VON BRAUN** वॉन ब्राउन

CRESCOGRAPH

RADIUM

RADIO

WIRELESS (RADIO TELEGRAPHY)

SIR JAGDISH C. BOSE जगदीश चन्द्र बोस   **MADAME CURIE** मैडम क्यूरी   **G. MARCONI** जी. मार्कोनी

THE COMPUTER

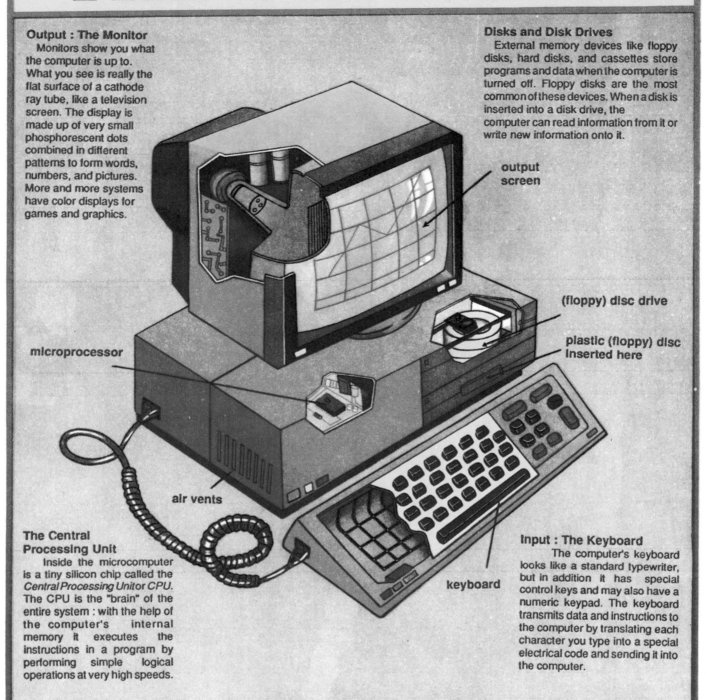

Output : The Monitor
Monitors show you what the computer is up to. What you see is really the flat surface of a cathode ray tube, like a television screen. The display is made up of very small phosphorescent dots combined in different patterns to form words, numbers, and pictures. More and more systems have color displays for games and graphics.

Disks and Disk Drives
External memory devices like floppy disks, hard disks, and cassettes store programs and data when the computer is turned off. Floppy disks are the most common of these devices. When a disk is inserted into a disk drive, the computer can read information from it or write new information onto it.

output screen

(floppy) disc drive

plastic (floppy) disc inserted here

microprocessor

air vents

keyboard

The Central Processing Unit
Inside the microcomputer is a tiny silicon chip called the *Central Processing Unit* or *CPU*. The CPU is the "brain" of the entire system : with the help of the computer's internal memory it executes the instructions in a program by performing simple logical operations at very high speeds.

Input : The Keyboard
The computer's keyboard looks like a standard typewriter, but in addition it has special control keys and may also have a numeric keypad. The keyboard transmits data and instructions to the computer by translating each character you type into a special electrical code and sending it into the computer.

THE COMPUTER HAS BEEN CALLED AN "ELECTRONIC BRAIN". THE REASON FOR THIS IDEA IS CLEAR. COMPUTERS CAN CALCULATE AND REMEMBER FACTS. YET A COMPUTER IS NOT A BRAIN. IT IS MERELY AN ELECTRONIC DEVICE THAT CAN PERFORM CALCULATIONS AT GREAT SPEED.

THERE ARE FOUR MAIN PARTS TO A COMPUTER. FIRST THERE IS AN INPUT DEVICE. THIS IS OFTEN A KEYBOARD LIKE THAT ON A TYPEWRITER. THE KEYBOARD IS USED TO GIVE INFORMATION AND INSTRUCTIONS TO THE COMPUTER. SECONDLY, THERE IS AN OUTPUT DEVICE. THIS IS OFTEN A SCREEN LIKE THAT ON A TELEVISION. IT SHOWS THE RESULTS OF THE COMPUTER'S WORK. THIRDLY, THERE IS THE COMPUTER'S MEMORY. ONE TYPE OF MEMORY IS CALLED A FLOPPY DISC MEMORY. THIS USES A PLASTIC DISC, LIKE A SMALL RECORD, TO HOLD INFORMATION. THE DISC IS INSERTED INTO A SLOT AT THE FRONT OF THE COMPUTER WHEN THE COMPUTER NEEDS THE INFORMATION HELD ON

THE DISC. THERE IS ADDITIONAL MEMORY INSIDE THE COMPUTER, IN THE FORM OF SILICON CHIPS. THESE ARE SMALL PIECES OF SILICON - ABOUT THE SIZE OF A CHILD'S FINGERNAIL - ON WHICH COMPLETE ELECTRONIC CIRCUITS ARE BUILT.

THE FOURTH IMPORTANT PART OF A COMPUTER IS A CHIP CALLED A MICROPROCESSOR. THIS DOES ALL THE CALCULATIONS AND CONTROLS. THE OPERATION OF THE COMPUTER. THE MICROPROCESSOR RECEIVES THE LIST OF INSTRUCTIONS - THE PROGRAM - WHICH IS TYPED ON THE INPUT KEYBOARD. THIS HAS TO BE TYPED IN USING A SIMPLE LANGUAGE THAT THE COMPUTER CAN UNDERSTAND. THE MICROPROCESSOR THEN DOES THE CALCULATIONS INVOLVED, CALLING ON THE MEMORY FOR ANY INFORMATION IT NEEDS. FINALLY, THE MICROPROCESSOR TELLS THE SCREEN TO DISPLAY THE ANSWERS TO THE QUESTIONS IT HAS BEEN SET.

INDEPENDANCEDAY

OUR NATIONAL SYMBOLS

Our National Symbols

These charts broadly document the diverse cultures and peoples of India, particular historical periods, religious and political leaders, industry and work. They are thematically varied, yet together, illuminate a fascinating projection of unity – the idea of a nation. Every facet creates a sense of a modern state and the symbols which stand in for a polity.

Paradoxically, their precursors go back to a period even before the birth of modern India in 1947. The *People of India* (p.79) owes its origins to 18th and 19th century colonial traditions of painting 'types': a man and his wife, in their best 'holiday' clothes, with the accessories of their status or trade. Later, ethnological surveys in colonial India classified the subject population into discrete racial, ethnic and occupational groups. Colonial knowledge systems followed a fairly neat categorisation: People of India, Tribes and Castes of India, Handicrafts of India. Interestingly, almost the same orientalist categories appear in the charts. Even when the eye is an Indian one, it still carries a vague exoticism that has little to do with the varied people of India as they really are.

People of India, with its outdated anthropological representations, seems particularly frozen in colonial time. Yet, the original classification is diluted by the happy randomness of the chart world, with a Nepali and a Christian couple thrown into the same scheme. Reckless as they are, charts inadvertently end up parodying a historical enterprise that has since been deemed megalomaniacal. Without the conscious knowledge of its earlier use, *People of India* transforms an originally cynical and politically suspect exercise into one which, though still suspect, is a charmingly proud display of cultural diversity.

Dances of India (p.81) and *Indian Handicrafts* (p.83) spring from the same impulse. In *Indian Handicrafts*, the notion of handicraft is stretched to include the modern professions of electrician, darner and turner, while still keeping the old Hindu caste-based categorisation of 'lowly' professions such as cobbler, potter and blacksmith.

Children of India (p.80) has its subjects dressed in adult clothes with the supposed accessories of their origin. A Christian boy helps the reader out by wearing a tie and holding a guitar. Yet the chart does not so much help to realistically identify or allow us to learn about others as to create a sense of Indian 'unity in diversity' – a favoured government slogan.

Our Helpers (p.84) seems to come from a clearer, more recent source – the post-independence sentiments of nation building, when the idea of India had to be defined for its citizens. It is a curious mix of images signifying a modern, progressive nation through the work that its citizens do. Agriculture, law, education and medicine form half of this model. The other half is given over to the armed forces and the police (see also p.133). Together they present a patriotism whose icons are noble work and the defence of borders. It is part of a set of charts that could be described as 'national-patriotic' that also includes *Industries of India* (p.88), *Reservoirs of India* (p.86) and *Satellites Launched by India* (p.87).

Several charts on work are included. While they could be read as merely presenting a range of occupations, they also undeniably frame the occupations in symbolic value. The farmer, for instance, like the soldier, is a recognised symbol of patriotic sentiment. *Farming* (p.85) makes characteristic use both of the traditional image of the bullock and plough as well as the progressive irrigation pump. A rural idyll of plenty, and technological progress, are the two sides of the nation building coin. Puzzling in its categories, but identical in its impulse is *Arts* (pp.90-91). It showcases traditional, classical forms such as dance and sculpture along with the modern progressive 'arts' of medicine and astronomy.

One chart that is strictly not part of the nation-building ethos, and could even be considered as undermining it, is *Simple Ways of Earning* (p.93). It stands poignantly apart in this idyllic company, featuring such occupations as 'Cold Water Seller', 'Hand-cart Pusher' and 'Boot Polish Man'. Sadly, it is the only chart that comes painfully close to the humble aspirations its users can realistically have. There is nothing intrinsically 'low' about these occupations, yet they are cruelly devalued in Indian caste-based society.

The more joyous *Festivals of India* (p.82) takes on the patriotic framing of information in typical chart style. In a sequence showing various religious festivals, the panel 'Independence Day' – with children saluting the national flag – is perhaps not completely accidental. It may well be the key to the whole, struggling to hold together the different religious festivals – Muslim, Hindu and Christian – which form the Indian understanding of secular identity.

Our National Symbols (p.78), though not particularly creative visually, is significant in that it captures the place of symbols in the Indian imagination. They communicate strongly in India, and icons, such as the face of a leader, are clothed with the history of memory, aspirations and identity.

National figures are central to patriotic rituals, and it is evident that chart makers take their leaders very seriously as *Leaders of India* (p.95) shows. There are at least twenty variations of this chart, and like a list of one hundred best books, the leaders keep changing according to taste or location.

Similar in form are the history charts *British Period* (p.96) and *Ancient Kings* (p.97), which are composed of an uninterrupted gallery of figures. History education in India is full of such particulars, with a bare minimum of explanation to justify their relevance. History itself is a string of names and dates to be committed to memory. This leads to a very curious historical sense, obsessed with detail, yet vague in its understanding of process.

A commonplace and dearly held sense of Indian identity is linked to this viewing of the past: the idea of a glorious pre-colonial antiquity, usually going back 2,000 years. This symbol of richness lives in the common imagination, often without any clear sense of period, time or events. *Indian Coins of the Past* (p.99) illustrates this endearingly with a set of large, gleaming and obviously ancient looking coins. The coins reveal nothing further about themselves though, with neither caption, name, or date to give them anything more than symbolic value.

There are rich historical antecedents behind the art of these of charts. *People of India* for example, has very clear stylistic echoes of Company Art – the commissioned paintings of the colonial East India Company. Company Art convention is to place a man and his wife (usually of a 'humble' profession) against an undisturbed background along with the dress and tools of their trade. Artists in South India added to this by drawing from their native Tanjore style of painting which has flat, ochre, blue and green backgrounds.

Another convention of portraiture is evident in the charts that feature personalities, particularly *Leaders of India*. Here the resonance is the tradition of hand-painted photographs. The artist uses a base image (a painting, when no photograph is available) and reworks it, sizing it to suit the dimensions of the chart. Some panels retain their studio origins, while others are transformed by paint to create a completely new image.

In *Ancient Kings* and *British Period* there are traces of the Mughal miniature style of flat rendering of profile. *British Period*, in particular, is striking in its absence of facial colour and brilliant use of white space and line to bring out expression and character.

The representation of women projects a certain feminine type from popular art, at once traditional and contemporary. Adorned in the modern sari, but proportioned according to aesthetic norms set out in classical Sanskrit texts, these women have full, round faces, flowing hair and permanently coy expressions. The *Women on Work* (p.92) chart is one of the few that shows women in a range of roles and professions, even though these professions remain fairly gendered. Women are almost always dressed in traditional clothes (except when they are in uniform), and their figures conform to the full-breasted, wide-hipped ideal that is typically found in Indian calendar art.

OUR NATIONAL SYMBOLS
நமது தேசிய சின்னங்கள்

National Flag

தேசிய கொடி

National Emblem

தேசிய சின்னம்

National Bird - Peacock (Mayur)

தேசிய பறவை மயில்

தேசிய கீதம்

ஜன கண மன அதி நாயக ஜயஹே
பாரத பாக்ய விதாதா
பஞ்சாப ஸிந்து குஜராத மராட்டா
த்ராவிட உத்கல வங்கா
விந்திய ஹிமாசல யமுனு கங்கா
உச்சல ஜலதி தரங்கா
தவசுப நாமே ஜாகே
தவசுப ஆஸிஷ மாகே
காயே தவ ஜய காதா
ஜனகண மங்கள தாயக ஜயஹே
பாரத பாக்ய விதாதா
ஜயஹே ஜயஹே ஜயஹே
ஜயஜய ஜய ஜயஹே

தேசியப் பாடல்
வந்தே மாதரம்
சுசாலம், சுபலம்
மலாயஷா, சிட்டாலம்
சாசியாசியாமலம், மாதரம்
சுப்ராஜியோஜுனா
புலகிதாயாநிம்
புலகுகமிதா
டிரமதாலா சோபினிம்
சுகாஷிளிளிம் சுமதுரா
பட்சினிம்
சுகாதம் வர்தம்
மாதரம்

National Anthem

Jana-gana-mana adhinayaka jaya he
  Bharatha-bhagya-vidhata.
Punjaba-Sindhu-Gujarata-Maratha-
  Dravida-Utkala-Banga
Vindhya-Himachala-Yamuna-Ganga
  Uchhala-jaladhi-taranga
Tava subha name jage,
  Tava subha asisa mange.
Gahe tave jaya-gatha.
  Jana-gana-mangala-dayaka jaya he
Bharata-bhagya-vidhata
  Jaya, he, jaya he, jaya he,
Jaya jaya jaya, jaya he.

National Animal Tiger (Panthera)

தேசிய மிருகம் புலி

NATIONAL SONG

Vande Matram !
Sujalam, suphalam,
Malayaja-shitalam,
Shasyashyamalam, Mataram,
Shubhrajyotsna,
pulakitayainim,
Phullakusumita-
drumadala-shobhinim,
Suhasinim sumadhura-
bhashinim,
Sukhadam varadam,
Mataram !

National Flower - Lotus

தேசிய பூ தாமரை

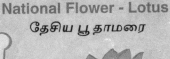

PEOPLE OF INDIA भारत के लोग

CHILDREN OF INDIA
भारतीय बच्चे

HINDU हिन्दू   SIKH सिख   MUSLIM मुस्लिम   CHRISTIAN क्रिस्चियन   HARYANA हरियाणा   GORKHA गोरखा

MADRASI मद्रासी   Uttar Pradesh उत्तर प्रदेश   GUJARATI गुजराती   BENGALI बंगाली   PUNJABI पंजाबी   MARATHI मराठी

NAGA नागा   BIHARI बिहारी   KASHMIRI काश्मीरी   Himachal Pradesh हिमाचल प्रदेश   RAJATHANI राजस्थानी   KERALA BOY केरल का बच्चा

DANCES OF INDIA

NATRAJ GARBA (Gujarat) BIHU (Assam) JHIMMA (Maharashtra)

DHANKOOT (Meghalaya) ANDHRA FOLK DANCE HARYANA FOLK DANCE BHANGRA (Punjab)

ORISSA DANCE HIMACHAL FOLK DANCE RAJASHTAN FOLK DANCE BHOOTKOLA (Karnataka)

MALI (M.P.) ROUF DANCE (Kashmir) NAGALAND FOLK DANCE KATHAK (U.P.)

BHARATA NATYAM (Tamil Nadu) SANTHAL DANCE (Bihar) KATHAKALI (Kerala) MANIPURI (Manipur)

FESTIVALS OF INDIA

DEEPAVALI

HOLY

IDD

PONGAL

CHRISTMAS

ONAM

INDEPENDANCEDAY

SARASVATHI POOJA

82

No. 147

SRI RAM, MADURAI.

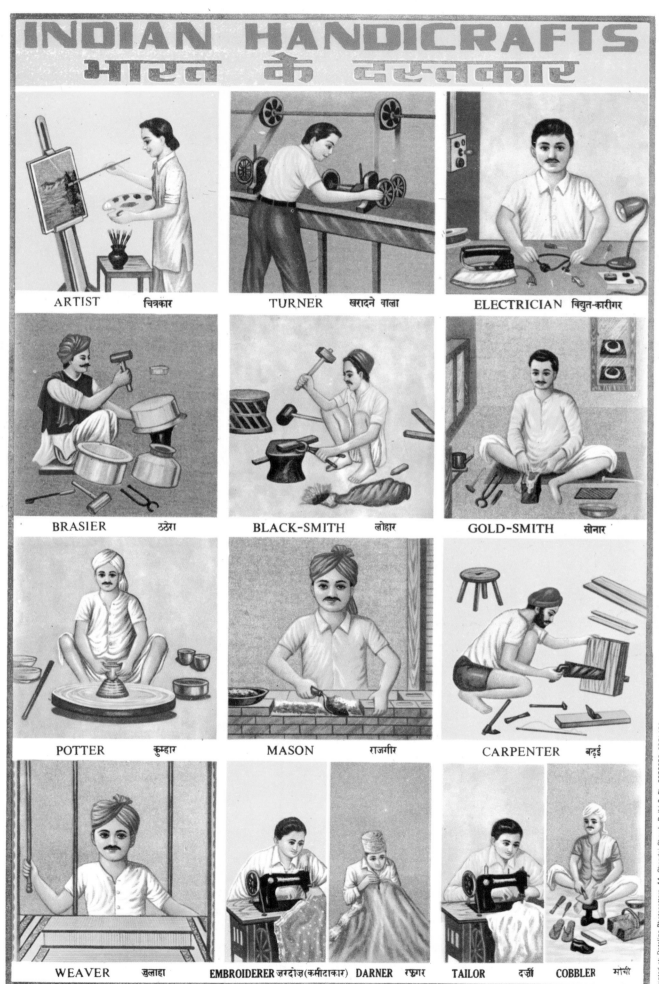

INDIAN HANDICRAFTS
भारत के दस्तकार

ARTIST चित्रकार

TURNER खरादने वाला

ELECTRICIAN विद्युत-कारीगर

BRASIER ठठेरा

BLACK-SMITH लोहार

GOLD-SMITH सोनार

POTTER कुम्हार

MASON राजगिर

CARPENTER बढ़ई

WEAVER जुलाहा

EMBROIDERER जरदोज़(कसीदाकार) DARNER रफ़ूगर

TAILOR दर्ज़ी COBBLER मोची

Published by: Indian Book Depot, Map House. Bahadur Garh Road Delhi-6.

83

OUR HELPERS
हमारे सहायक

SHIPCAPTAIN

ARMY

PILOT

TEACHER

FARMER

ADVAGAT

POLICE

SOLDIER

HOME GUARD

NURSE

DOCTOR

TRAFIC POLICE

FARMING

PLOUGHING

Sri Ram Madurai

TRANSPLANTING

WATER LIFTING

SPRAYING

HARVESTING

THRUSHING

WINNOWING

GRAINS STORAGE

STORING

66

RESERVOIRS IN INDIA

HIRAKUD - ORISSA

BHAKRA - PUNJAB

RIHAND - U.P.

GHANDISAGAR-RAJASTHAN

VAIGAI - TAMILNADU

KRISHNARAJA SAGAR MYSORE

MALAM PUZHA - KERALA

PEECHI - KERALA

Sri Ram 46. Therkkuvasal Chinnakkadai Street, Phone No. 33982 Madurai-1.

86

58

EARTH SATELLITES LALINGHED BY INDIA.

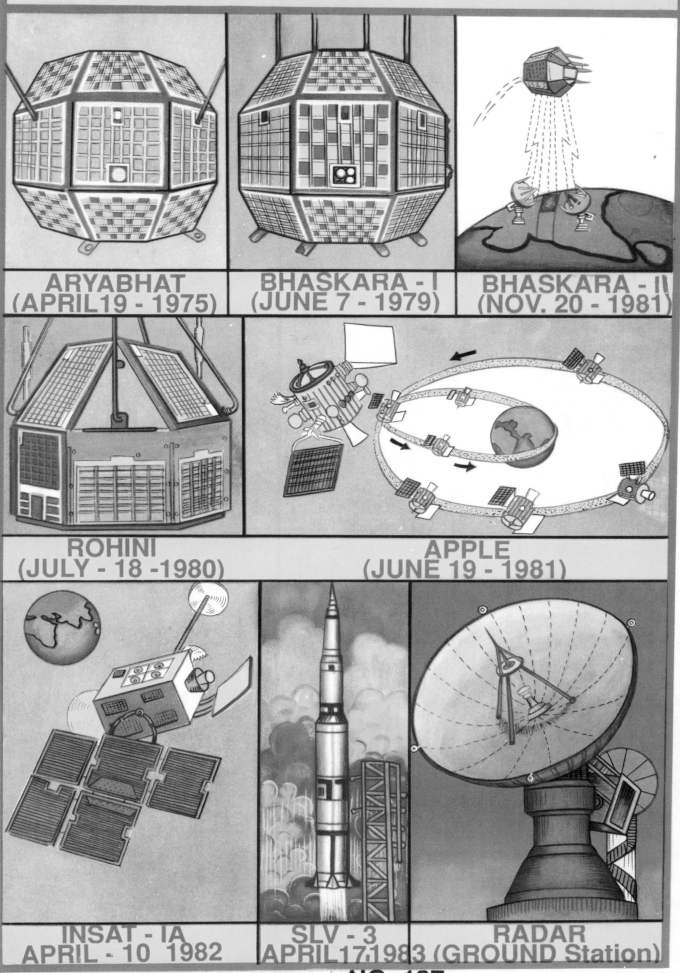

ARYABHAT
(APRIL19 - 1975)

BHASKARA - I
(JUNE 7 - 1979)

BHASKARA - II
(NOV. 20 - 1981)

ROHINI
(JULY - 18 -1980)

APPLE
(JUNE 19 - 1981)

INSAT - IA
APRIL - 10 1982

SLV - 3
APRIL17,1983

RADAR
(GROUND Station)

Sri Ram Madurai

NO. 137.

87

ROCKET PAD, THUMBA

LIGNITE CORPORATION, NEYVELI

HINDUSTAN STEEL PLANT, ROURKELA

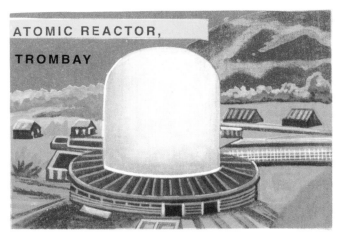

ATOMIC REACTOR, TROMBAY

HINDUSTAN AUTOMOBILES, BENGAL

HINDUSTAN AIRCRAFT, BANGALORE

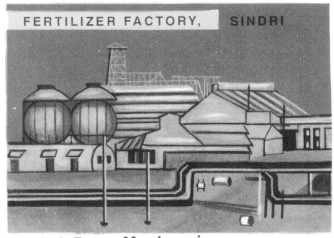

FERTILIZER FACTORY, SINDRI

STEEL PLANT, DURGAPUR

TYPES OF WORKERS WORKS :- தொழிலாளியும் – தொழிலும்

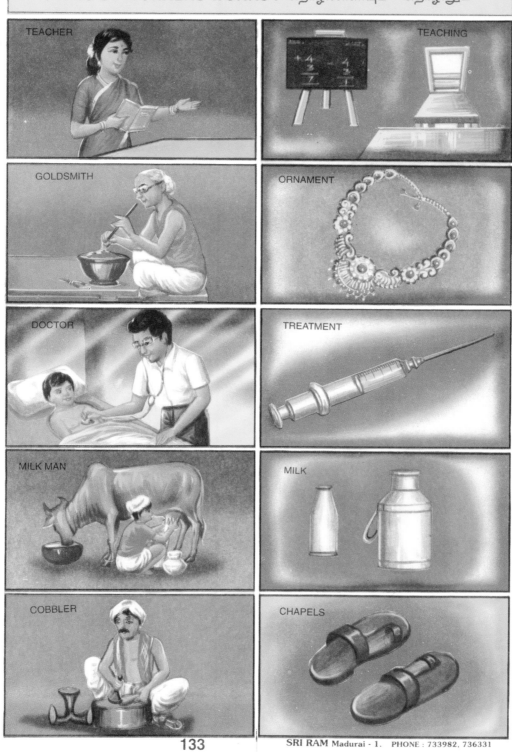

TEACHER	TEACHING
GOLDSMITH	ORNAMENT
DOCTOR	TREATMENT
MILK MAN	MILK
COBBLER	CHAPELS

133

SRI RAM Madurai - 1. PHONE : 733982, 736331

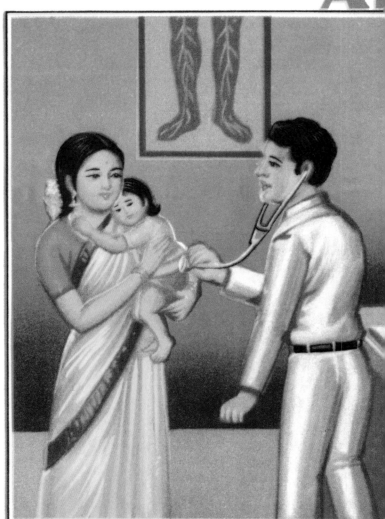

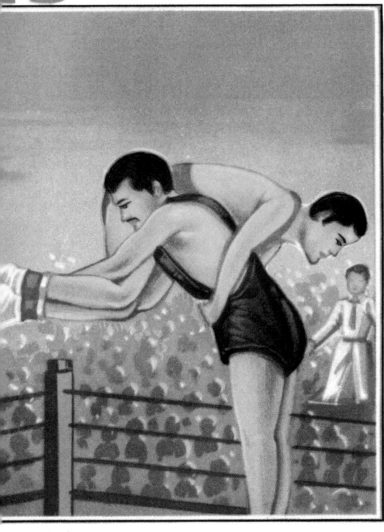

WOMEN ON WORK

COOKING WORK

FARMING

TAILORING

AIR HOSTESS

TELEPHONE OPERATOR

OFFICE SECRETARY

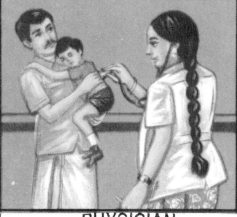

PHYSICIAN

NURSE

TEACHING

122 PAINTER

MUSICIAN

SPORTS GIRLS

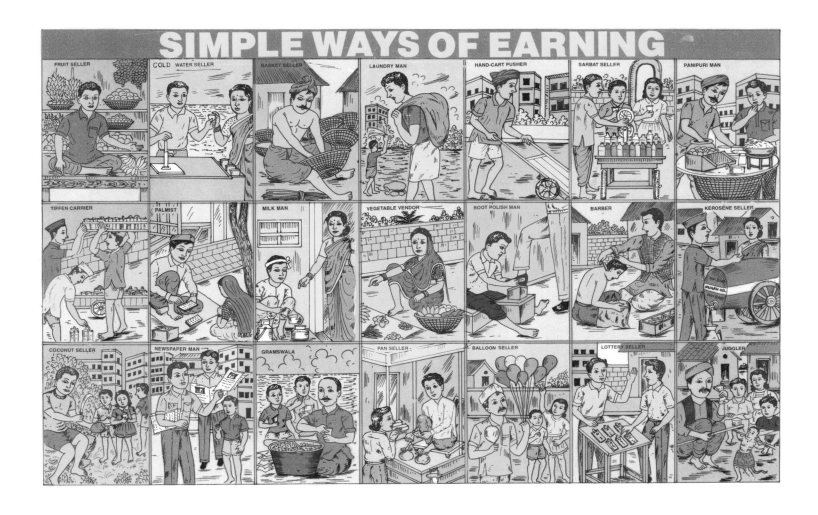

93

दक्षिण अफ्रीका का सत्याग्रही गाँधी, 1914

गाँधी जी, 1920

जेल यात्रा, 1932

महात्मा गाँधी

बैरिस्टर एम.के. गाँधी, 1907

दांडी का नमक सत्याग्रह, 1930

मोहनदास करमचन्द गाँधी और कस्तूरबाई का विवाह, 1881

अंग्रेज़ो, भारत छोड़ो! 1942

विद्यार्थी मोहन, 1880

बापू और जवाहर, स्वतन्त्रता प्राप्ति–15 अगस्त, 1947

राष्ट्रपिता महात्मा गाँधी
1859–1948

मोहन का जन्म, 2-10-1869

बापू गाँधी

गांधी जी की समाधि राजघाट, नई दिल्ली

निधन 30 जनवरी, 1948.

LEADERS OF INDIA CHART No. ⬤

Gopal Krishan Gokhale

Lokmanya Tilak

Lala Lajpat Rai

Pt. Madan Mohan Malvia

Subhash Chandra Bose

Mahatma Gandhi

C. Rajagopalachari

Dr. Rajendra Prasad

Dr S. Radhakrishnan

Dr. Zakir Hussain

V. V. Giri

Fakhruddin Ali Ahmed

N. S. Reddy

Shri Zail Singh

Pt. Jawaharlal Nehru

Sardar Patel

Lal Bahadur Sastri

Morarji Desai

Smt. Indira Gandhi

Shri Rajiv Gandhi

95

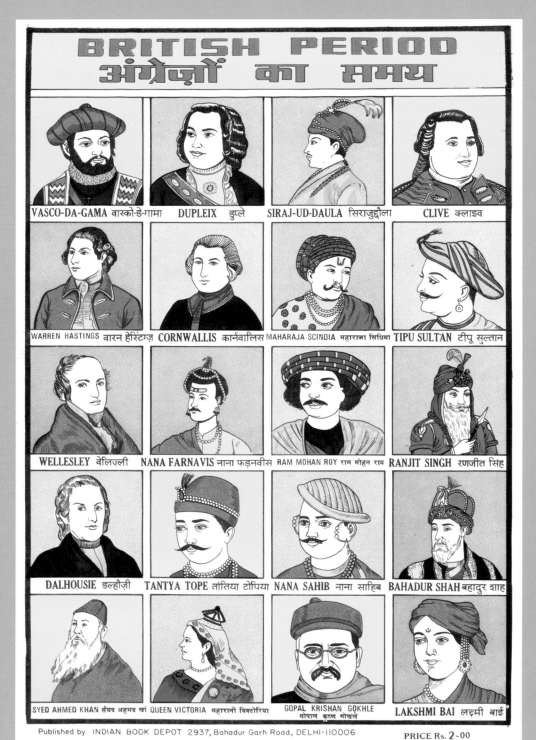

ANCIENT KINGS

ASHOKA • CHANDRAKUPTA • POURAS • VIKRAMADITYA
KRISHNADEVARAYA • SANAKKIYA • RAJARAJAN • PRUTHVIRAJ
AKBAR • RANAPRADAP • SHAJAHAN • BABAR
SHIVAJI • TIPUSULTAN • NANA PHADANVIS • AURANGZEB
RAJARAM MOHAN RAI • RANJIT SINGH • BAHADURSHA • QUEEN OF JANSHI

SRI RAM Madurai - 1.   PHONE : 733982, 736331

NO. 77

97

GREAT TEACHERS OF INDIA भारत के महान पथ-प्रदर्शक

Maharishi Valmiki   महर्षि वाल्मीकि

Ved Vyas   वेद व्यास

Gautam Buddha   गौतम बुद्ध

Mahavir Swami   महावीर स्वामी

Samrat Ashok   सम्राट् अशोक

Adi Shankracharya   आदि शंकराचार्य

Ramanujacharya   रामानुजाचार्य

Sant Gyaneshwar   संत ज्ञानेश्वर

Guru Nanak Dev   गुरु नानक देव

Chaitanya Mahaprabhu   चैतन्य महाप्रभु

Sant Namdev   संत नामदेव

Samrath Ramdass   समर्थ रामदास

Aurobindo Ghosh   अरविन्द घोष

Raja Ram Mohan Ray   राजा राम मोहन राय

Dayanand Saraswati   दयानन्द सरस्वती

Ramkrishna Paramhansa   रामकृष्ण परमहंस

Swami Vivekananda   स्वामी विवेकानन्द

Swami Ramtirtha   स्वामी रामतीर्थ

Swami Shraddhanand   स्वामी श्रद्धानन्द

Mother Teresa   मदर टेरेसा

PRINTERS: MUKHPRAKASHENGRAVER, NARAINA, PH. 5796554

INDIAN COINS OF THE PAST

பழங்கால இந்திய நாணயங்கள்

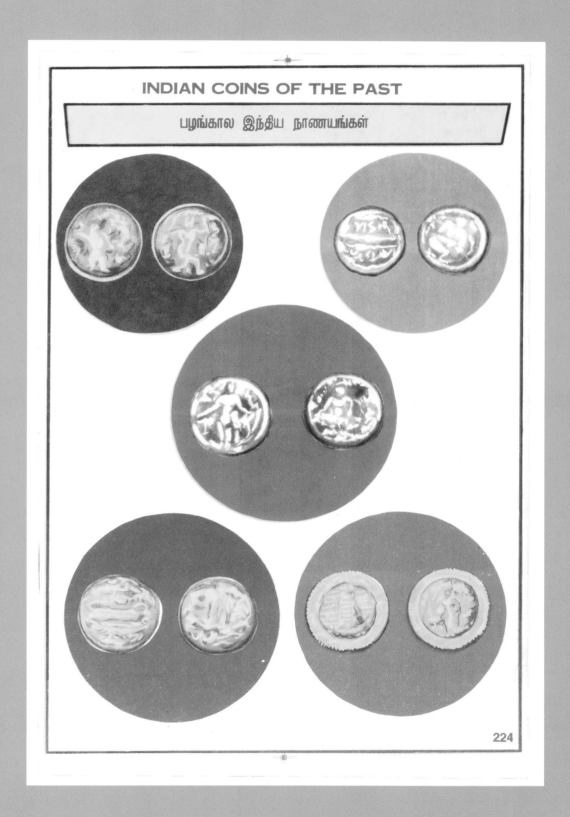

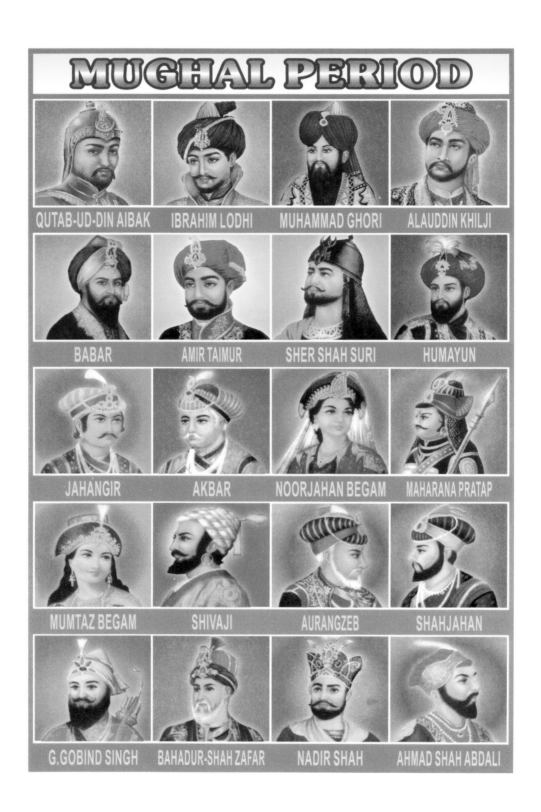

MUGHAL PERIOD

QUTAB-UD-DIN AIBAK	IBRAHIM LODHI	MUHAMMAD GHORI	ALAUDDIN KHILJI
BABAR	AMIR TAIMUR	SHER SHAH SURI	HUMAYUN
JAHANGIR	AKBAR	NOORJAHAN BEGAM	MAHARANA PRATAP
MUMTAZ BEGAM	SHIVAJI	AURANGZEB	SHAHJAHAN
G.GOBIND SINGH	BAHADUR-SHAH ZAFAR	NADIR SHAH	AHMAD SHAH ABDALI

NO. 004

WONDERS OF
THE WORLD

WONDERS OF THE WORLD

People of the World (p.105) is probably the most deliciously outrageous chart in this set. It connects to *People of India*, both in form and content and although there is a direct kinship between the two *People of the World* has a different dimension. *People of India*, creates a sense of the self, whilst *People of the World* sets up an image of the 'other'. It is this sense of the alien and the exotic that brings this small but important set of charts together.

They focus on the marvels of a world foreign to their audience, content to stay with stereotypes. *People of the World* is likely to strike most people as one of the most absurd and politically incorrect of the charts, but its stereotypes are not intended as vicious misrepresentations. They are really inexcusable and ill-informed gaffes, originating from a certain artlessness. Located in a pre-politically correct worldview, they re-work the received stock of popular understanding, and in this sense at least, they are innocent.

The most direct link to education practice is the so-called Seven Wonders of the World, part of history lessons for middle-school children. In the *Wonders of the World* (pp.103-104) the Wonders have grown from the original seven to an unstable ten or sixteen, which change from chart to chart. Their names are memorized and recited almost like a liturgy, turning them into iconic objects unconnected to place or time. In the broadest sense, these charts stem from a sensibility curious about unknown worlds. It is a special kind of interest shown by ordinary people in India, who have no real access to foreign places or life in these lands. Images of the foreign are consumed as fantasy, seldom confused with actual possibilities in the real world. The foreign locale, person or object is a visual stand-in for an emotion, a kind of a stock-image conveying romance, glamour and the excitement of difference.

Indian cinema plays on this, and is responsible to a great extent for creating and feeding the fascination for the exotic. Romantic song and dance sequences are set in glamourous settings such as Singapore, the Swiss Alps, New York or London. The foreign is essentially a sentimental trope, signifying abundance, beauty, or style. Iconic in function, these images are not invested with truth or accuracy, and with no focus on the particular or the historic, they can be mixed together at will.

It is this popular feeling for the icon that also governs the group of charts: *Leaders of the World* (p.109), *Inventors of the World* (p.110) and *Religions of the World* (p.111).

These are not strictly exotic themes, although they deal with the non-Indian world. Simultaneously familiar and global, they are a way of universalising Indian notions of history and personality. The even-handed acceptance of all the religions of the World, for instance, reiterates the Indian sentiment of tolerance of all religions.

Leaders of the World also possesses a distinct resonance in Indian popular culture. Some of the leaders evoked in these charts – Ivan (the Terrible), Garibaldi, Napoleon, George Washington, and even Hitler – may surprise the outsider. The origins of this gallery go back to the freedom struggle against the British, when they were given the status of heroes in the popular imagination. What united them, and made them relevant, was that in one way or another, they represented a politics of defiant nationalism and a passionate love for their land. Others, like Stalin and Lenin, are part of the distinctive icons created by the communist movement in India, and no Leaders' chart is complete without them. To this day, it is not unknown to give their names to children. The present Mayor of Chennai city is called M.K. Stalin.

The two forms of this set of charts – the exotic and the iconic – are reflected in the art as well. The representations of the exotic are composed almost entirely of stock models. In the nameless people of the world chart (p.106), all racial types are cast in one mould, with only Bowler hats, straw headgear, Nehru caps or Stetsons to tell them apart. They seem to come from another time, like all the other *People of the World*.

In fact, they do. The history of this particular form of representation can be traced to colonial education. The widely available children's magazines of the 1920s and 1930s regularly featured such types under the column 'Our Friends in Other Places'. Written into the legacy of colonial education, they continued to be one of the sources for the propagation of cultural stereotypes. The second kind of human portrait, used in *Leaders of the World* and *Inventors of the World* tends more to realism and accuracy. Mainly hand-painted photographs and re-worked stock images, they hint at an authenticity, which is nonetheless teased back into the chart world by the artist's hand.

WONDERS OF THE WORLD
संसार के आश्चर्य

The Colossus of Rhodes (Bronze Statue of Apollo) रोड्स का कलोसस (अपोलो देवता की विशालकाय कांस्य मूर्ति)

The Tomb of Mausolus मॉसोलस की समाधि

The Great Pyramid of Khufu खुफु का विशाल शंकु-आकार मीनार (पिरामिड)

The Pharos of Alexandria सिकन्दरिया का फेरोस (नाविक मार्गदर्शक प्रकाश-गृह)

The Hanging Gardens of Babylon बेबीलोन के लटकते बाग़ (हैंगिंग गार्डन्ज़)

The Temple of Diana at Ephesus एफ़ेसस में डायना देवी का मन्दिर

The Statue of Jupiter Olympus ओलम्पस पर्वत पर ज्युपिटर की मूर्ति

The Great Wall of China चीन की बड़ी दीवार

Taj Mahal, Agra ताज महल, आगरा

The Empire State Building, New York एम्पायर स्टेट बिल्डिंग, न्यूयॉर्क

Eiffel Tower (Paris) आइफ़्रल टावर, पेरिस

The Colosseum (Rome) कोलोसियम, रोम

The Leaning Tower of Pisa पीसा का झुका हुआ मीनार

The Statue of Liberty, New York लिबर्टी (स्वतन्त्रता देवी) की मूर्ति, न्यूयॉर्क

The Stonehenge (England) स्टोनहेंज इंगलैण्ड

The Statue of Christ of the Andes एण्डीज़ पर्वत पर ईसा मसीह की मूर्ति

103

WONDERS OF THE WORLD

THE GREAT PYRAMID OF KHUFU

MAUSOLEUM AT HALICARANSSUS

TAJ MAHAL

HANGING GARDENS OF BABYLON

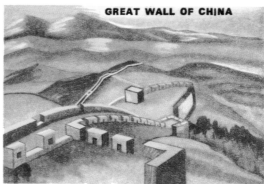

GREAT WALL OF CHINA

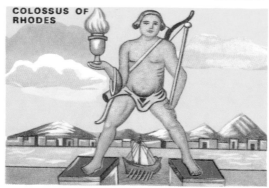

COLOSSUS OF RHODES

TEMPLE OF ARTEMIS

PHAROS OF ALEXANDRIA

LIBERTY STATUE (U. S. A.)

STATUE OF ZEUS

Sri Ram Madurai

83

PEOPLE OF THE WORLD

AMERICANS

RUSSIANS

JAPANESE

FRENCH

ENGLISH

PAKISTANIES

CHINESE

ARABS

BURMESE

RED-INDIANS

ESKIMOES

KIRCHESE

PATHANS

BALINESE

PIGMIES

NEGROES

105

AFRICAN

INDIAN

CHINESE

ENGLISHMEN

ARABIAN

RUSSIAN

NO: 123

106

 India

 Tibet

 Indonesia

 Samoa

 Thailand

 U.S.A.

 Egypt

 Africa

 Arizona

 China

 Iran

 Japan

 Russia

 Germany

 England

 Greenland

SRI RAM. MADURAI.

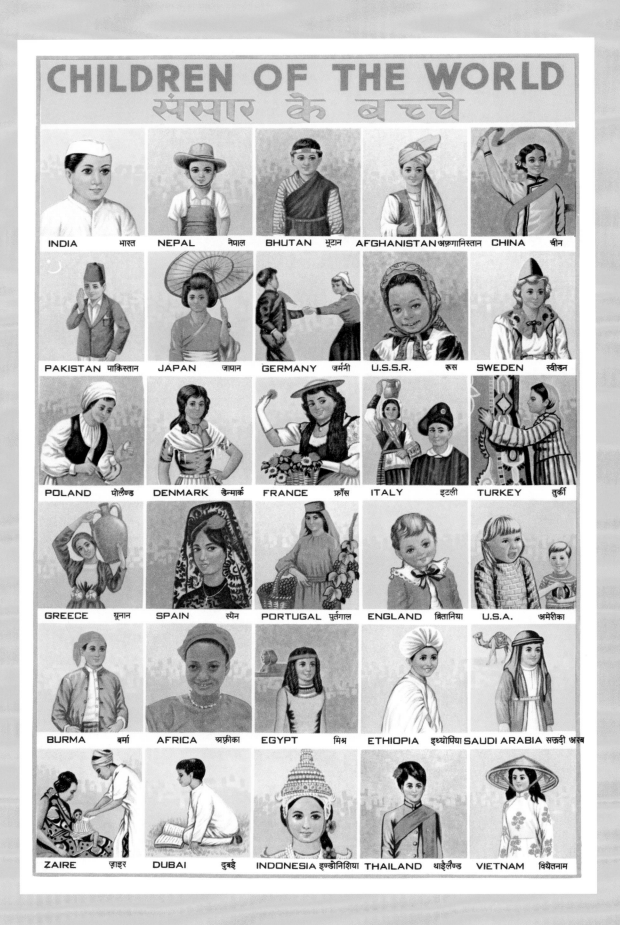

LEADERS OF THE WORLD

CHARLES MACNE

ROBESBERRY

LINCOLN

CROMWELL

RICHELUE

HITLER

LENIN

STALIN

NAPOLEON

CHURCHILL

CARDINAL

ALEXANDER

BISMARK

ROOSEVELT

NASSER

MAO-TSE-TUNG

ATILLA

HENRY VIII

ANIBAL

JOAN OF ARC

CARIBAI DI

IVAN

TYMUR

KATHANARAN

MUHAMMAD II

CAESAR

LOUIS XIV

WASHINGTON

CHENKIZ KHAN

MUSSOLINI

109

Published by : FRIENDS OFFSET CALENDARS. "CHART HOUSE" 39, BUNDER STREET, MADRAS - 1. PH : 589419, 562372.

GREAT INVENTORS OF THE WORLD.

GALILEO
TELESCOPE

FARADAY
ELECTRO-MAGNET

STEPHENSON
STEAM ENGINE

L. PASTEUR
BACTERIA

VONBROWN
ROCKETS

WILBER WRIGHT
AEROPLANE

EDISON
MOVING PICTURE

L. VINCI
CAMERA

BAIRON
TELEVISION

BENJAMINFRANKLIN
LIGHTNING

CARATHORS
NYLON

VOLTA
VOLTICPILE

MARCONI
RADIO

GRAHAMBELL
TELEPHONE

FLEMING
PENICILLIN

HARVEY
BLOOD EIR CULATION

S. MORSE
TELEGRAPH

GUTENBERG
PRINTING

JENNER
VACCINATION

NOBLE
DYNAMITE

Sri Ram 46, Therkkuvasal Chinnakkadai Street,
Madurai - 1.

RELIGIONS OF THE WORLD

HINDU TEMPLE	GURUDHWARA	MASJID	CHURCH
PRAGATHI POOJA	HAWAN YANGA	LORD SHIVA (HINDUISM)	LORD BUDDHA
SRI MAHA VEER (JAIN)	JESUS CHRIST	PAGODA (CONFUSIUS)	ATHINA (VIJAY AND YUNANI DEVI)
SRI GURU NANAK (SIKH)	MAHATMA JARTHUSHTRA (PARSI)	SAMRAT ASHOKA	AKBAR
SRI GURUGOBIND SINGH (SIKH)	HAJRATH MOHAMEED (ISLAMISM)	JAI HIND	MAHATMA GANDHI (AHIMSA)

GREAT PHILOSOPHERS

BUDHA

JESUS CHIRIST

ELANGHO

THIRUVALLUVAR

VIVEKANANDAH

BHARATHI

MAHAVEER   No 118

KAMBAR

SRI RAM 46, Therkkuvasal, Chinnakkadai St., MADURAI-1.

CAMEL

NO. 005

SOME OCCASIONS

SOME OCCASIONS

CRADLE CEREMONY

MARRIAGE FUNCTION

SCHOOL CAMP

TONSURE FUNCTION

GRAHA PRAVESH FUNCTION

BIRTH DAY PARTY

FAMILY PICNIC

SRI RAM ZOO CHART

116

OUTDOOR GAMES

Hockey

Cricket

Football

Basketball

Judo

Baseball

Boxing

Wrestling

YOGASAN CHART

PASHCHIMOTANASAN	BHUJANGASAN	Urdhaw Sarvangasan	Sarvangasan (Halasan)
KARNPIRASAN	SHALBHASAN	DHANURASAN	USHTRASHAN
CHAKRASAN	JANUSHIRSHASAN	TRIKONASAN	MATSAYANAN
MAYURASAN	GOMUKHASAN	Ardhmat Syendrasan	BHADRASAN
BADHPADMASAN	SHIRSHASAN	UTTANPADASAN / SHAVASAN	PADMASAN

119

MEANS OF RECREATION

PICNIC SPOT

ZOO

OUTDOOR GAMES

TELEVISION

HILL STATION

CINEMA

CIRCUS

AMUSEMENT PARK (APPU GHAR)

VIDEO PARLOUR

INDOOR GAMES

RADIO

THE VEHICLES COMING FORM RIGHT
SIDE TO PROCEED STRAIGHT FORWARD

NO. 006

**SOURCES OF
COMMUNICATION & ARTS**

Charts and Educational History

In their immediate use, charts answer the needs of an educational system directed at acquiring and retaining large collections of facts. The majority of schools in India evaluate their students through examinations that test their ability to memorise and reproduce – rather than understand – information. Acquired largely for its own sake, information is iconic, existing almost as superstition.

The Origins of Modern Education in India

Modern Indian education grew out of two interlinked histories – colonial rule and missionary endeavour. India's British rulers viewed education in essentially moral terms – as a means to civilise the subject races of India, and to convince them of the inevitability of British rule. Learning, for Indians, was to be concerned primarily with facts, and to work consciously against the seductions of the imagination.

The actual content was underwritten by material needs. The British needed loyal native assistants to mediate between themselves and a diverse population. The mediators turned out to be largely from the Brahmin and other upper castes, and the British worked out a curriculum for them which would feed directly into the business of government. For this class of Indian, they chose English – rather than Indian languages – as the medium of education, since it alone had the power to deracinate them.

Information played a crucial role in this scheme, involving innumerable details of civil life. Such an education rapidly became prized, and endowed with a certain worldly value – diligent pupils found good jobs in the government.

Through the mid to late 19th century, the British supervised the setting up of institutions of public schooling. In addition to this, existing local schools became common schools. Teachers were trained to communicate the new curriculum to their pupils – arithmetic, geography, the physical sciences and English literature. The sciences were to counter native irrationality, whilst English literature was to fulfill the important role of humanising the native.

Textbooks were in English, though in poorer schools, the vernacular remained the medium of instruction. But even this vernacular was changed from the regional dialect to a new, artificial and homogenised master language, free of the inflexions of everyday speech and context. This language found its way into textbooks as well and students were tested through examinations which demanded answers be recalled verbatim.

The main impact of this, and of the standardised textbook, was that learning ceased to be contextual. In pre-colonial times, most education was practical and local, essentially linked to a profession. The negative side of this was its inherent inequity, since professions were tied to caste and a rigid social hierarchy. Although the standardised colonial textbook brought a kind of democracy into educational practice, its contents were more often than not irrelevant. A peasant child, under the new system, had to learn about the geography of England, the achievements of Lord Clive and the names of Roman Emperors. Unsurprisingly, colonial schools alienated many, and found less and less pupils from the peasant and working communities.

But not all children suffered. Students from the elitist upper castes, especially Brahmins, adapted fairly well to the new system. Traditional Brahminical knowledge was already based on rote learning and abstractions. The ability to memorize lengthy sacred and philosophical texts – and recite them with a precise intonation – was highly prized. Brahmin students drew on their mnemonic past to remember and reproduce information – however abstract and fantastic – in a manner that suited the pedagogic and political intent of their rulers. It is not surprising that of those students who survived high school and went on to study in colonial universities, Brahmins were in the majority.

These were the people who later went on to write the textbooks. Convinced of the twin ideals of information and instruction, they privileged fact over context, and instruction over comprehension. The content remained English in inspiration, while practice was informed by Brahminical methods. This integration of Brahminical pedagogy within a colonial educational system produced a curious and – for the majority – oppressive hybrid.

Missionaries at Work

Meanwhile, British and European missionaries fed into dominant educational thought with their own version of morality and sanctimony. Active in the field of education, their philosophy scorned mere secular learning and warned of the evils of excessive rationality and free thought.

Both the colonial government and the Indian elite were wary of their intentions. So the missionaries concentrated to a large extent on schooling the very poor – the so-called 'untouchables' and lower castes. Here they discovered a willing, though bewildered, constituency thankful for the modest missionary schoolroom, and for a faith that did not seem to discriminate on the basis of caste. Missionary schools were also attractive because they taught in the local language, and frequently combined textbook teaching with imparting practical trade skills.

Teaching in these schools was laced with Christian fervour, and directed as it was at the very poor, obsessed with hygiene and good habits, connecting them to moral worth. Students were exhorted to lead the good Christian life, a kind of proselytising that was also evident in the publications that missionaries produced for adults and children.

Education Now

Education in contemporary India bears the impress of these distinctive legacies. The idea of school as a place where children memorise facts and have morals preached at them continues to haunt Indian education. Learning is still associated with social prestige, less to do with conceptual progress and more with information gathering. Honourable and taxonomic, it is a rhetorical, rather than an educational enterprise.

As for textbooks, the dual concern with information and instruction survived British rule into independent India. Early nationalist thinkers were both critical and admiring of colonial pedagogy – angered by its irrelevance, but drawn to its promises of progress and modernity. The text-books of independent India addressed contemporary anxieties over identity and knowledge within a framework of national freedom, praising India's past, the freedom struggle, its techno-logical ambitions and the vitality of its democracy. These facts were relevant to the learner's context only because they were contemporary concerns. But they were still taught in the abstract.

In the final analysis, nationalist educationalists were more force-ful in their repudiation of colonial education than in imagining a different system for free India. Very few questioned its basis: information and instruction. And with the exception of Gandhi, they did not address the average pupil's lived context, which was never considered enabling. All Indian children became recepta-cles into which 'standard' urban school wisdom – considered inherently progressive – was to be poured. Worse still the exami-nation system became even more crucial. An exam was the gate-way to a career, a job in government, or promotion in the ranks.

Contemporary learning still follows the imperatives of memory and recall. Textbooks are packed with facts, some updated, others anachronistic. Science books fare better in this respect than those for English or History. History textbooks, for example, continue to draw on material produced in colonial times, and students commit to memory all sorts of dates, personalities and unexam-ined racial assumptions. The language of English readers does not draw from the energy of the spoken tongue, relying instead on a quaint and outmoded form of Englishspeak, particularly evident in the government run schools for poorer children.

Charts emerge, at the end of this brief history, as a poignant sym-bol of what education means to the mass of Indian children. This is tempered only by the thought that at least with this mechanical approach, the inputs children receive may not sink in too deeply.

In their favour, it may be said that charts possess a visual and popular dynamism, largely absent in Indian educational circles. They detect schoolroom demands faster than policy makers ever do, and most importantly, they are responsive to the touching good faith of a people deeply convinced of the value of a literacy founded on garnering facts, however dubious their usefulness.

Charts and the History of Popular Art

The modern Indian city thrives on visual conversation. The Indian imagination invests a great deal in images, from decorated shop shutters and painted wall fronts to giant cinema hoardings. The chart artist himself is a practitioner of several of these forms and charts, with their striking visuals and bold colours, belong to this milieu.

What unites this range of graphic mediums is that they are functional. They are linked to the marketplace, and reliant on public demand – although this is not to ignore that they reflect other impulses.

Tracing the informing principles behind the art of charts involves examining the antecedents of popular art itself, and the evolution of the urban artist. Unlike the field of education, where clear-cut, documented changes in policy and practice offer clues for interpretation, this is a history that has few established markers. It can perhaps be most fruitfully picked up at a point in time when significant changes took place in the market for art.

New Patrons
In the late 18th century, with the coming of the British to India, an important change took place in the world of the artist. The basis of patronage shifted from local community and royal support, to a more dissipated, uncertain one, in which the artist took his chance in the open market.

Local economic and community life was drastically transformed as kingdoms were conquered or became protectorates, where kings ruled in name only under the surveillance of the British. With their financial affairs no longer under their complete control Royal patrons could not afford to be generous.

Demand for art, however, was not at an end. The new patrons were British soldiers, adventurers and the 'nabobs' of the English East India Company – a giant mercantile concern that more or less ruled India until the Crown officially took over in 1858. But the existing work did not alto-

gether satisfy the needs of this new elite. One soldier described Indian drawings of the time as "done in the delicate and laboured manner of the miniature, though they are at the same time entirely devoid of truth in colouring and perspective and constantly err on the side of ornament and gaudiness of dress".

What the British were looking for was fresh content in a form already known to them – naturalistic records of picturesque places and lifestyles. Though naturalism was not a style of depiction known in India, market pressures were such that the British were able to actively assert their normative assumptions of good taste – and see them realised.

Company Art
The British set about commissioning artists to portray them in their new exotic settings, and to paint pictures of the country and populace of India. Initially a small group of European artists supplied this demand. Gradually, displaced Indian court artisans took over, tutored by the British in the naturalist tradition. Not only traditional painters, but also potters, carpenters and goldsmiths learnt skills like shading, perspective and line, to create the kind of images that could be taken home to England as mementoes.

New themes began to be considered worthy of representation and wide consumption. These models simultaneously guided the consumer as to what was worth coveting, and introduced the artist to visual approaches to meet this demand. Many of the forms that originated at this time continued to live on in subsequent popular art, taking on different impulses and structures of feeling with each passing period.

Indian art began to be overlaid with British style. Still retaining the flavour of their traditional skills, Indian artists assimilated their lessons to create a unique and hybrid form that became known as Company Art, after the East India Company.

Company Art convention was to take local themes with picturesque content: an Indian man and his wife, trades and professions, local fruits, strange birds, or tropical plants. Rendered in a

muted, naturalistic style, the images were a significant change from the devotional paintings of the previous century, using watercolours rather than gouache, and often discarding the brilliant hues of Indian miniatures for soft blues, sepia and green. Yet they never completely took on the western realist mode. Keeping some of their flat colours and ornament based aesthetic, artists gave Company paintings an exotic touch with a distinctly local hand. Demand for this art grew and was later supplemented by other, more local clientele. Educated Indians, taking on British mannerisms and attitudes, ordered similar artifacts for their homes.

Company Art was practised in its original form from the late 18th to around the mid 19th century. Later, its aesthetics and impulses were absorbed – and further hybridised – into other popular styles which also developed their own distinct audiences.

Early Photography

When the Crown took over rule from the East India Company in 1858, India became officially part of the British Empire. The unequal relationship between the rulers and their subjects was now more sharply defined, within a clearly articulated ideology of racial and political dominance.

It was from this position that the famous Risley survey of Indian anthropological types was conducted between 1868 and 1875. The exhaustive eight-volume survey took as its subjects the people of India – a theme that Company Art had already touched on – in a different way. The Risley survey was a census, documenting the trades, castes and professions of India through the new medium of photography. But the difference was more than just the medium. While Company Art themes were an assertion of an orientalist aesthetic impulse, the survey's intentions were to govern and control the Indian population, in an administrative and military sense, as well as a visual one.

Over time, the ideology of anthropological documentation filtered into the older aesthetic norms of Company Art. It created its own system of knowledge about the people of India, as well as defined ways of seeing them. These were carried into other spheres, written into textbooks, and into the vocabulary of photography itself. Of course, not everyone who wielded a camera did so in the service of the Empire, but the anthropological framing of Indian subjects became a defined genre.

The camera came to India as early as 1840, just one year after Daguerre invented it. It was not just the British who used the camera – some Indians took to it quite easily as well. A growing Indian elite – nobility and merchants in the service of the British Raj – also formed part of the emerging clientele for photography.

An interesting thing happened to the medium in Indian hands. While the framing of photographs remained more or less within the reigning scheme, the finished image turned away from the stiff realism of the conventional photograph, into an older aesthetic. Prints were frequently painted over by hand, to combine both realist and painterly qualities. Clothes were retouched with colour, and ornamentation, facial highlights, and settings brushed in.

Some British photographers also used this technique, which seemed to return something of the local colour that was not captured through black and white photography. The image moved away from being a 'true' representation and became part painting, part photograph, requiring both modes of seeing from the viewer. This technique was to have important resonances for the vocabulary of an emergent popular graphic art in India.

Bazaar Art

Painting continued to be commercially viable throughout the 19th century, and resonances of Company Art were reflected in local styles. As the general market for this art expanded, a new type of urban artist emerged, who did not necessarily have specific patrons. As his growing clientele became more amorphous, the themes grew wider, and more subjects proved commercially viable. The milieu of these artists was the bazaar or general market-place.

Several kinds of bazaar artists flourished during this period. The famous Kalighat School of painters from Bengal, for instance, comprised potters and carpenters who also painted scrolls in the pre-British days. They now began to paint on paper. Influenced by European notions of perspective, they freely adapted western framing devices for their full, rounded images which clearly owed their volume to their earlier potter's craft. They also took in new images being produced around them in late nineteenth century Bengal, from lithographs, stage settings and woodcuts. Kalighat painters were in touch with the contemporary, and captured topical tales of sex, religious corruption and murder.

Around this time, the barrier between 'high' and 'low' art began to blur. Even oil painting, hitherto a 'high' art form, was taken up by bazaar painters and sold to wealthy Calcutta homes. Kalighat painting continued to flourish throughout the 19th century, until cheap lithographs and oleographs began to flood the market in the late years of the century. The form then dwindled, although the very last Kalighat painter produced work until 1930.

The Shekhawathi painters in western India responded to a different set of conditions. Shekhawathi was home to wealthy merchant families, many of whom migrated to Calcutta in the 18th and 19th centuries to make their fortunes in the new colonial trading centre. They brought back examples of the new art, including Kalighat paintings, and commissioned local artists to paint similar scenes for them.

Shekhawathi artists were largely stonemasons, draughtsmen and itinerant craftsmen from various parts of northwestern India. Using their employers' descriptions of English life, and whatever other visual references they had, the artists painted fantastic murals on the walls of opulent homes. Their reference sources were eclectic – Kalighat paintings, English newspapers, litho prints, packing case labels, or cigarette boxes. Murals in Shekhawathi homes

feature Englishmen engaged in 'typical' English activities such as driving a motorcar, or listening to a gramophone. Here too, as in the work of Kalighat painters, older traditions mixed with the new. One of the Shekhawathi artists painted three Europeans passing around a hookah in a garden of grapes and pomegranates – a characteristic motif of Mughal and Rajasthani miniatures.

The artists of Shekhawathi also had other introductions to European aesthetic conventions. In the later half of the 19th century, Colonel Boileau, a well-know military man, passed through the region and presented one of the painters with a 'Camera Lucida', which projected an image on a screen. Boileau also introduced them to the foreign art of full-face portraiture. Indian painting traditions, especially Mughal and Rajasthani miniature styles, favoured the flat profile, rather than the three dimensional face. This new way of depicting the human face appears to have impressed the artists of Shekhawathi. One of them created an excellent portrait of Boileau, and several went on to draw full, rounded faces in their murals.

In South India, the bazaar artist had different local traditions to fall back on. The Company school had flourished here from the 18th century onwards, not only in colonial Madras, but also in the older temple towns of Trichinopoly, Madurai and Tanjore. Tanjore in particular was famous for its ornate, strikingly coloured religious paintings. The old form took on newer techniques such as shading, to produce depth and three-dimensionality while still retaining original elements of colour, ornament and perspective. In the late 19th century, this mixed style with its intelligent use of chiaroscuro was particularly evident in portraiture.

Marking the emergence of popular art with a wide appeal, the sites of artistic production multiplied rapidly during the 19th century. Apart from painting commissioned work and bazaar pieces, artists were sought out to decorate all sorts of surfaces: matchboxes, labels to be pasted on cloth-bales, travel trunks, or tea boxes. They used a variety of images, from gods and goddesses of Hindu mythology to faces of locally known heroes, workmen

of different trades, typical English pastimes, festival scenes, and ferocious animals.

Lord Napier, Governor of Madras, actively directed Indian artists to take up European techniques, believing that Indian legends, landscapes and people would be better represented by rendering them realistically. Napier even suggested specific themes for the Indian artist – the steps of the village tank, cattle in rice fields, crowds at religious processions, and mourners returning from the cremation ground.

The Legacy of Ravi Varma (1848-1906)

One of the most pivotal figures in the history of Indian popular art – who consciously used these themes and techniques – was not strictly a bazaar artist. He was Raja Ravi Varma, a painter in the court of the Maharajah of Travancore in southern India, one of the few principalities that still retained artistic patronage as late as the end of the 19th century.

Varma learnt the European techniques of perspective, shading and the naturalistic style in his youth, and began to render Indian themes in this way. His work – now considered by some critics as 'high' kitsch – nonetheless aspired to the status of classical or 'high' art, in the European fashion.

With his acquired mediums of canvas and oil, Varma went on to create a distinctive style that evoked romantic and idealised images of India's spiritual past. Against Renaissance-style landscapes, he placed gods, goddesses, heroes and heroines from literature and ancient theatre, Some of his subjects were secular, many derived from recognisable classical themes of Western painting. Because of the high quality of his workmanship, and the strong Western influence, his work was popular with European audiences.

But the movement that gave his art its iconic meanings came from another source. The period in which Ravi Varma worked was a time of great flux for the Indian sensibility.

There was a rise in nationalist feeling among educated Indians, associated with a growing unease and indignation over the inequities of British rule. The figures that Ravi Varma painted were perceived among his growing local clientele as embodying glorious, age-old qualities, which all Indians could be proud of. His use of western realism endowed scenes from the epics and Hindu heroes with a certain 'reality', that brought the past into the present.

Ravi Varma took this further by painting early leaders of the nationalist movement, and expressed his intention of creating a picture of India by painting a series of women from different regional types. While his broad documentary resembled the earlier 'People of India' themes, the spirit of the times covered the exotic with the mantle of the ideal. Although subject and form were not unlike what had gone before, the impulse that created and received them was new. To disseminate his work, Varma started his own printing press, and with the new technology of lithography, affordable prints of his paintings reached thousands of Indian homes.

The iconic and representative status of Ravi Varma's art marked the emergence of the popular as a demand created by shared structures of feeling. Although he died in 1906, his work continued to gain in popularity through the early twentieth century. As the nationalist movement grew, it was taken up by a constituency who valued his art for more than just aesthetic or commercial purposes.

Further popularisation of the Ravi Varma style came through scores of imitations. Until well into the twentieth century, lithographs of mythic representations of gods and goddesses, as well as Indian heroes and heroines in romantic landscape settings were produced in large numbers and distributed all over the country. This kind of mass imitation and use further collapsed the differences between the 'high art' that Ravi Varma aspired to, and bazaar art. Their iconography was carried on into what became known as calendar art – popular images of gods and goddesses on daily calendars, used in most Indian homes even today.

< L Match Box Cover, 1920s
< R Book Cover, 1940s

Early Urban Graphic Art

Even as Varma's work gained a singular popularity, other hybrid bazaar art forms continued to be resilient, finding new commercial arenas in which to exist and grow. In the early decades of the 20th century, along with paintings and religious oleographs, work was also to be found in the emerging areas of advertising, magazines, signboard painting and packaging.

The new work was produced on a variety of media – canvas, paper, walls, tin, cardboard and cloth. Apart from those who kept with the Ravi Varma tradition, the urban artists of the early and mid 20th century cannot easily be identified with any particular tradition or school, unlike the distinctive painters of Company Art, Kalighat and Shekhawathi. They all carried shades of the forms that went before them. Impulses and models travelled, either through patrons who bought different kinds of paintings and held them up as examples worthy of emulation, or through the new print medium that had a wide distribution system.

The urban artist was essentially a nomad, casting about for work, taking his cue from the demands of the market place or his patrons. He learnt his art through apprenticeship, or sometimes just by observing older practitioners and taking what he chose of their technique. Mostly, the artist learnt through improvisation, to answer quickly to wider and more disparate needs.

From the 1930s onwards, it is interesting to turn to the south, and Tamilnadu in particular, where some of the most vibrant popular art movements in India have their origin. Printing presses, especially in the town of Sivakasi, near the old Temple city of Madurai, were starting to flourish.

Throughout the last quarter of the 19th century, and well into the early decades of the 20th, artists found other work that suited their skills. Along with backdrops for studio photography, popular Tamil proscenium theatre – with its

origins in the 1860s – called for elaborately painted sets. The relatively new form of cinema in the 1930s increased this demand. Artists who worked with these newer forms still retained memories of the narrative of temple murals, the colour of folk rituals and rural landscapes.

Throughout the 1940s, as the British prepared to leave India, the indigenous market for popular art expanded. Local language publishing and the printing industry grew substantially to feed an audience that was exclusively Indian. The word 'popular' now addressed a very different set of tastes and needs.

C. Kondiah Raju (1898-1976)

One of the artists who travelled with the theatre groups of the 1920s and 1930s was C. Kondiah Raju. A distinct figure in the more generalised progress of urban graphic art in South India, Raju studied European and Indian styles of painting as well as the new discipline of 'commercial art'. He painted sets and backdrops for drama troupes until he settled down in the town of Kovilpatti, near Sivakasi which was already a growing site of printing activity and which expanded to include large-scale offset printing in the 1950s.

Here Kondiah Raju made his special contribution to popular art. He began by turning his hand to all kinds of graphic tasks, from painting metal boxes and traveling trunks to producing lithographs for calendars. But what made him famous were his 'framing pictures' – paintings of Hindu deities that were framed and hung in prayer rooms. With the spurt in the offset process, Kondiah Raju's very distinctive 'god paintings' became a common household feature.

Raju's work is practically the model on which religious calendar art is based to this day. Because his style has been so completely appropriated by his disciples and others who followed, it is difficult today to comprehend its uniqueness. Though influenced by the work of Ravi Varma, Kondiah Raju nevertheless created something very clearly his own, which he considered his aesthetic and spiritual vocation. But unlike Varma, who aspired to western realism in the formal sense, Raju kept the ornate, bejeweled

A Goddess, Framing Picture
C. Kondiah Raju, 1950s L >
Woman with a Sickle, Magazine Cover
K.Madhavan, 1960 R >

quality of classical Tanjore painting. His borrowing from the western realist tradition was the three-dimensionality and human fullness he gave his characters.

It is likely that he was inspired by his experiments with photography and hand-painted photographs. Raju had started his own photo studio, where he worked on photographs to create an authentic but non-realistic result. The final image that he used in his paintings was closer to the idealised sculptural form than to a human individual, a mode of representation that fed through into calendar art.

Raju's involvement with theatre sets came through in the flat, painted backdrops against which he placed his characters. Much like actors in a play, they were framed by curtains, pillars and arches, with painstakingly rendered drapery and props. These conventions – bequeathed to calendar art by Kondiah Raju – proved to be abiding ones.

K. Madhavan

Another unique – almost antithetical – impulse came from a contemporary of Kondiah Raju. Considered the 'Norman Rockwell' of South India, K. Madhavan learnt from his uncle, an ivory carver. Unlike Raju, he was not drawn to the religious, but deliberately turned to secular subjects, creating a thematic and visual break in the world of popular graphic art.

Madhavan's secular world-view stemmed from his involvement in a dissident political movement. The largely agnostic non-Brahmin Dravidian movement (1916-) of Tamilnadu challenged the Hindu religious and caste system. One result of this was a questioning and weakening of the links between religion and the arts.

Madhavan's art was wide-ranging. Painting contemporary scenes of rural life, he produced visual archetypes of ordinary people: the farmer, the worker, the village beauty, the peasant's wife and the local political notable. Madhavan's skill endowed these stock figures with the energy of popu-

lar feeling, always keeping them on this side of banality. His work found its way to the public through postcards, posters and the covers of popular Tamil magazines.

He also painted realistic portraits of the Dravidian movement's leaders that became so popular that they came to possess an iconic value. Almost all politically aware 'lower' caste homes in the 1950s possessed prints of his portraits.

Like Raju, Madhavan had begun his career in the early decades of the twentieth century, painting scenic backdrops for theatre groups. When cinema came, he went on to design and paint film sets. The growing appeal of cinema was fortuitous to the Dravidian movement's own secular and aesthetic concerns, and Madhavan was attracted to the energies of the film world, which provided both the content and the tropes for an exciting graphic style. He also made posters and banners, using photography overlaid with strong colours to create a dramatic and fabulous quality. His most prolific work was in the 1950s and 1960s, which was also the most creative period for this kind of urban art.

Interestingly, Madhavan's art responded to non-Indian film traditions as well. He seems to have achieved his distinctive style of characterisation through scrupulous observation and imitation of Holywood film stills, which, of course, he Indianised.

Madhavan could be considered one of the last distinct individuals in the anonymous world of popular art. His style was mimicked by those who followed, becoming a point of reference for artists in the secular tradition. Other talented artists succeeded him, but it is too early to say which of their work will survive.

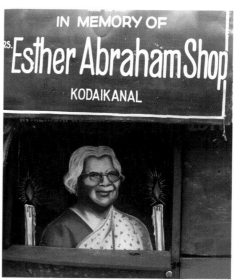

< Facing Page: Political Wall Painting

Hand-painted Traffic Sign L >
Shop Signboard R >

Below
Religious Unity Message, Wall Painting >

The Urban Popular Artist Today

These points of reference highlight the larger movements in the course of Indian popular art during the last two hundred years. But the narrative is not a linear one. No new impulse breaks completely with previous forms, and each successive style carries memories of those that have gone before it. Some of these memories are visible in their original form, while others are layered over, or transformed into new modes.

The tropes created in the 1960s have proved resilient practically into present times. The images of today still carry qualities that defined the art of thirty years ago, though materials like vinyl and plastic are now more widely used, and the quality of printing has improved vastly. Hand-painted, individual work continues to exist alongside the mass print medium, and most commercial manufacture is still small-scale. The contemporary urban artist is also

not unlike his 19th century predecessor who came to the city in search of work, from a village or small town. He is a displaced artisan or a self-taught nomad, willing to work with new media, but never really letting go of his relationship to tradition. He works with handed-down conventions that he both inherits and subverts through improvisation.

What really has changed is the canvas of the artist – which is now the city itself. Increasingly, the best graphic art is found in the public spaces of ever more crowded Indian cities. Walls and streets are the most visible and cheaply available spaces for contemporary urban art – advertisements, messages, posters and political graffiti. Laws that regulate city spaces struggle to enforce discipline, and the Indian city has become visually garrulous in an unprecedented way. In a largely non-literate society, the visual is accorded a great deal of importance. Popular images assume a certain potency, and with their omnipresence and lively energy, actually appear to subvert the world of the literate. In this sense,

131

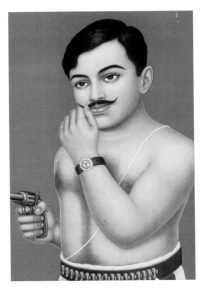

each message the urban artist creates is as much a form of expression as it is a means to survive.

Carrying millions of individual voices, the Indian city is an anarchic but curiously democratic space, and it is this unwitting democracy that makes it so vibrant.

Chart Art

Charts are a unique form of this family of energetic art. They first emerged in the 1950s, in response to a need for simple, colourful and inexpensive teacher training aids. In the 1970s, when offset printing became more advanced, charts became even cheaper and more widespread. With their bright colours and strong visuals, they were easily accepted in the classroom, and stayed very much within this context.

Although charts are distinct in their form and use, the chart artist also paints walls, billboards and signage. He does not specialise in the chart form, but brings his skills to it in the same way that he contributes his voice to the streets of the city.

The artist's techniques and inspirations are defined by the long history of popular art: Company Art, Ravi Varma's paintings, Madhavan's portraits, English magazines from the 1950s, hand-painted photographs – all of which comes down to him as a visual and stylistic legacy. More conscious inspirations are taken from references that he is exposed to: early children's encyclopedias, textbooks, mythological comics, and magazines. Chart publishers generally keep a stock of such reference material, much of which dates back to another period or context. The artist draws from these sources, but his local and personal inflections are always visible beneath the borrowed visual syntax.

Because the same hand does a variety of work, modes of rendering seep in and out of all the graphic forms that the chart artist creates. Charts carry the boldness of posters, the drama of wall paintings, and the elaborate stage sets of cinema. Conversely,

chart art can be seen in traffic signs, calendars, wall
plaques, advertising, posters and cinema hoardings.

What allows the chart to draw from all these elements and
retain its uniqueness as a form, is the focus that the chart
artist must have. The pulling together of all the varied
elements is a function of context, combining ideology and
art within a given grid. When the artist takes on the final
representation of this, he remixes the various forms at his
command into something unique.

Acknowledgments

We wish to thank Trotsky Marudu and Indrapramit Roy for their suggestions and observations on popular urban art in India, S. Theodore Baskaran, Gnani, Dilip Kumar and Indu (Madras Craft Foundation) for their help in sourcing original art work, R.Natarajan for sharing his memories of K.Madhavan.

Art Credits

A Toddy-tapper and his wife, Madras, 1785 and *Jockeys, Kalighat* – Courtesy of the Trustees of the V&A, London.
English Soldier in Shekhawathi – Avinash Veeraraghavan's photo collection
Royal Couple, Photograph by Federico Peliti – Peliti Associati
Ravi Varma's *Girl on a Swing* and K.Madhavan's *Woman with Sickle* – Roja Muthiah Research Library, Chennai, India
Mythological Comic Panel, from Amar Chitra Katha Title, No. 534, *Bheeshma* – India Book House Limited
All prints and photographs, unless otherwise mentioned – Tara Publishing's Visual Archive, Chennai, India

Photo Credits

Photographs of Ravi Varma's *Girl on a Swing* and K.Madhavan's *Woman with a Sickle* by S.Theodore Baskaran
All other photographs by Sirish Rao, Avinash Veeraraghavan and Helmut Wolf

Select Bibliography

Archer, Mildred *Company Paintings: Indian Paintings of the British Period*, India Art Series, Victoria and Albert Museum, 1992
Bhattacharya, Sabyasachi (ed.) *The Contested Terrain: Perspectives on Education in India*, Orient Longman, 1998
Cooper, Ilay *The Painted Towns of Shekawathi*, A Mapin Guide to India Series, Mapin Publishing Pvt. Ltd, 1994
Goswamy B.N, *Feeding the Imperial Image*, The Tribune, Chandigarh, October 8, 2000: *Cameras and Colonial Encounters*, The Tribune, Chandigarh, April 30, 2000
Inglis, Stephen R. *Suitable for Framing: The Work of a Modern Master*, in *Media and the Transformation of Religion in South Asia*, edited by Lawrence A Babb and Susan S. Wadley, Motilal Banarasidass, 1997
Jain, Jyotindra *Kalighat Paintings: Images of a Changing World*, Mapin Publishing Pvt. Ltd, 1999
Rosser, Yvette Claire *Hegemony and Historiography: The Politics of Pedagogy*, The Asian Review, Spring 2000, Dhaka
E.M.J.Venniyoor, *Raja Ravi Varma*, The Government of Kerala, India, 1981

First published in the United Kingdom by
Dewi Lewis Publishing
8 Broomfield Road, Heaton Moor
Stockport SK4 4ND, England
+44 (0)161 442 9450

www.dewilewispublishing.com

Produced in assocation with Tara Publishing, Chennai, India

For the text: Sirish Rao, V. Geetha, Gita Wolf
For this edition: Dewi Lewis Publishing

ISBN: 1-899235-83-3

Printed in Italy by EBS, Verona

The authors and the publisher wish to thank

India Book Depot, Delhi
Sri Ram Industries, Madurai

for their generous permission to reproduce
the charts featured in this book.

I.B.D.
Charts
For Budding
Kids

(24 x 37 Cms. Size)

A collection of more than 100 colourful
PICTORIAL EDUCATIONAL CHARTS
on various subjects.

These charts are helpful to children in doing their home-work and also stimulate their imagination and simultaneously teach them fascinating facts about the world around them.